Light Factory

- A complete five-day holiday club programme for 5–14s
- Christ centred
- Bible based
- Full notes for teaching and discussion
- Drama scripts
- Activity leaflets
- Craft and game ideas
- Notes on presentation of the programme
- Daily Bible notes for team meetings
- Ideas for a family event

A lively, colourful programme presenting Jesus, 'The Light of the world'.

1. THE LIGHT OF THE WORLD
John the Baptist proclaims who Jesus is.

2. AN ENCOUNTER WITH THE LIGHT
A Samaritan woman finds that Jesus knows all about her.

3. A CONVERSATION WITH THE LIGHT
Jesus listens to and talks with Mary and Martha at Lazarus' tomb.

4. AN EXPERIENCE WITH THE LIGHT
Peter discovers how much Jesus loves him.

5. BELONGING TO THE LIGHT
Jesus' light still shines today.

HOLIDAY CLUB RESOURCE MATERIAL

Many people have contributed to the ideas in this programme, which has been put together by members of Scripture Union's Missions and Education in Churches departments

SCRIPTURE UNION
130 City Road, London EC1V 2NJ

Please note: Publicity material designed especially for this programme is available from the Christian Publicity Organisation, Garcia Estate, Canterbury Road, Worthing, West Sussex, BN13 1BW.

Reprinted 1992, 1993

British Library Cataloguing in Publication Data
Morgan, Janet
Light Factory.
1. Children, Christian religious education
I. Title. II. Flynn, Angela III Scripture Union
268.432

ISBN 0 86201 688 6

The Lighthouse drama serial is based on a script originally written by Vanessa Wick and adapted for use in this programme. The scenario was written by the Footprints Theatre Company.

Designed and illustrated by Tony Cantale Graphics
Cover illustration: Eira Reeves

Phototypeset by Input Typesetting Ltd., London.
Printed in England by Ebenezer Baylis & Son Ltd, The Trinity Press, Worcester and London.

Contents

Introduction

The LIGHT FACTORY combines a lively, fast-moving, colourful up-front presentation of Bible teaching, music, drama and various participatory elements, with small-group activities designed to build relationships between the children and leaders and aid children in their understanding of what is presented from the front. The programme is modelled on the lively, fast-moving 'magazine' programmes often seen on children's television. LIGHT FACTORY originated from a programme run by Scripture Union at a large Christian conference and has since been revised and adapted for use as a five-day holiday club programme.

LIGHT FACTORY LOGO

The LIGHT FACTORY logo should be used to raise the profile of the holiday club in publicity material. Use it within the club, too – on the hat, on stage, etc, to give the children a sense of belonging and identity as a group.

OVERALL AIM

To explore what is meant by Jesus' statement, 'I am the Light of the world'. This will primarily be done by looking at a number of people with whom Jesus came into contact and showing how those who belong to Jesus reflect his Light.

SETTING

A factory where we learn about a very special light. In the LIGHT FACTORY children are called *factory workers*, leaders are *supervisors*, and small groups called *factory units*.

Units should be made up of ten to twelve children plus one or two adults. Those units with younger children or that have leaders involved in some occasional up-front role (drama, music, key character, etc.) will need two leaders to ensure proper supervision. The children are assigned to units at the beginning of the week and stay in the same unit throughout. Children should be placed in units with other children from their particular age group, ie 5–7s, 8–11s, 12–14s.

It is best if the children are seated informally on the floor in their units with unit leaders sitting with them. If chairs are used, each unit should be arranged in a semi-circle facing the front. The units should have numbers which can be displayed so they can be seen easily by the presenters up front. These could be on large cards hung from the ceiling. The units may be placed in different areas of the room on different days so that the same units are not always at the front or back. You will need to keep in mind, though, that the younger children may have difficulty seeing over the heads of older children and thus may always need to be placed nearer the front.

Sets and properties

The stage and factory area should be decorated to look as much like a factory as possible, but much brighter! Carpet tubes covered in aluminium foil are very effective, as are boxes with dials painted on or levers attached, children's climbing frames etc. A large sign with LIGHT FACTORY on it should be made and hung at the back of the stage along with a large banner with the words:

Jesus said 'I am the Light of the world.'

It would be helpful to have a large clock face (at least one metre in diameter) with elements of the programme written around the circumference of the dial and one large hand to point to the element in which the children are presently involved. This helps build the atmosphere of anticipation each day and gives the children an idea of what sort of things they have to look forward to. All of the 'on-stage' items – sign, banner, clock, etc – should be very bright and colourfully done. The use of reflective card or foil, fairy lights, etc, will add to the brightness.

It is a great advantage if the stage area can be lit with stage lights which can be dimmed and flashed at appropriate times during the programme. The presentation is enhanced if a proper public address system is used and presenters use microphones. Disco lights coupled to the public address system will also be effective, as will the occasional use of blue or green flashing hazard lamps. You may need to hire or borrow special equipment for sound and lighting. Check with the local youth and community centre for ideas for a local supplier. (The programme is not dependent on sound and lighting but is enhanced by it.) If using special lighting and sound equipment it is best to ensure that the electricity supply and wiring in the venue is adequate to cope with the demand.

PROGRAMME PARTICIPANTS

The foremen
One or two people are needed to co-ordinate the overall running of the LIGHT FACTORY. They are normally more mature people who have no up-front or small group responsibility but are free to maintain oversight of the proceedings and respond to any problem that may arise. These are known as the foremen.

Presenters
The programme is led throughout by two or three presenters. One presenter should be designated as the one who keeps the programme to time, deciding when to cut short any items or add time to other items during the programme. Items dealing with the aim of the day, such as the *Walk-ons* and *Spotlight*, should not be cut. Other items can be cut short to enable the programme to finish on time. Presenters will need to be attentive while children are involved in small group work in order to know when the majority of units have finished and the up-front presentation should resume. They are responsible for ensuring that the aim is emphasised throughout the programme and not just during the 'teaching time'. They 'carry' the programme, making the vital links from one item to another. They are not responsible for leading a factory unit. The presenters always lead the main theme song and may also lead the singing of other songs. They could have special names relating to light such as *Lizzie Laser, Nicky Neon, Flora Escent, Ultra Violet, Sue Strobe*, etc, and wear special factory costumes such as white boiler suits, metallic fun wigs and flashing 'disco' headbands. These can be obtained from novelty shops.

Hints on Bible reading with children

Should we encourage under–10s to read the Bible? Yes! God can and does relate directly to children, and as they read his word they will begin to discover this for themselves. So the primary reason for encouraging under–10s to read the Bible is not just to give them a knowledge of its contents, but to enhance their relationship with Christ.

DO make sure that the children are familiar with the skills that are needed for reading the Bible eg:
- using the index
- finding a reference
- the difference between Old and New Testaments
- the distinctions between book/chapter/verse

DON'T assume that because a child can read, s/he can understand what is being read.

DO make it fun and exciting. If Bible reading is seen as 20 minutes' hard slog, the child won't attempt to do it once the activity is over.

DON'T make the 'fun' of Bible reading dependent on either the leader or the rest of the group being present. They won't be there when the child is at home!

DO give the children a booklet that will help them carry on Bible reading when they are on their own: *Find Out* for 5–7s; *Quest* for 7–11s; and *One to One* for 10–13s.

DON'T assume that the child will have access to a Bible at home. Is there any way your activity can help such children?

DO help them to see that Bible reading isn't just another 'chore' to be done, but that it is one way they will continue to learn more about Jesus.

DO let them know that *you* read the Bible and learn more about Jesus from it! Your enthusiasm will affect their attitude towards the Bible.

Below are ideas for how to organise three meetings for those children who want to find out more about Jesus through the Bible.

SESSION 1

Aim
To ensure the group knows what makes the Bible different from other books and why reading it is important.

Equipment
A Bible per group member.
Comics/newspapers/novels.

Method
1. Ask the group what they like reading and why they read it. (You may learn from this which of your group have reading problems.)

2. Talk about the Bible – it's different from any other book/comic etc – because:

a) it tells us about God.
b) it tells about what people are like and how God wants us to live.
c) it shows us how we can get to know God and become his friends.
d) God speaks to us as we read the Bible. (How will readers know what God is saying?)

Check
that your group can tell you (in their own words) why the Bible is special and why reading it is important.

SESSION 2

Aim
To teach the group how to use the Bible; to find book, chapter and verse.

Equipment
A Bible per group member.
A list of verses to find.

Method
1. Talk about the Bible as a library of books and how the contents page shows where these books are. (Explain briefly the division into Old and New Testaments.)
2. Get the group to open their Bibles somewhere in the middle.
3. How is the Bible different from other books? (All the numbers!) Explain how each book is divided into chapters (the numbers in large type) and verses (the numbers in small type). This is done to help them find the place they want.
4. Spend some time finding verses. (You could turn it into a game, eg sword drill.) Stop as soon as the group can find their way round the Bible more easily.

SESSION 3

Aim
To show the group how to read the Bible using an aid (*Find Out* for 5–7s; *Quest* for 7–11s; *One to One* for 10–13s).

Equipment
A Bible per group member.
Pencils/pens/Bible aid.

Method
1. Explain that reading the Bible is exciting but it isn't always easy. That's why we pray (talk to God) before we start.
2. Show the group the Bible reading aid you will be using. Explain how it works, how it will tell them which part of the Bible to read and how it will help them understand what it is saying.
3. Get them to do the day's reading on their own or with a partner. Watch out for those who are having problems with reading/writing etc.
4. If they can, ask them to tell the rest of the group something they have discovered. (But don't force it!)
5. Pray. Tell God about these discoveries.

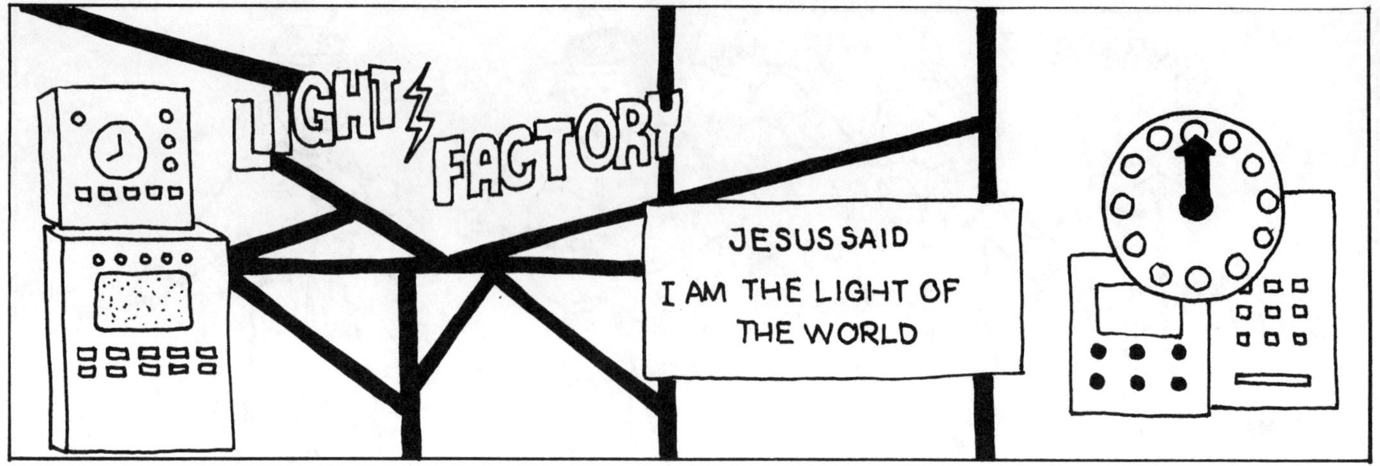

Stage backdrop

Key character
The Bible story is told through the key characters each day. They are 'introduced' through a number of surprise 'walk-ons' at the beginning of the programme. A different person will be needed each day to portray the character(s) as they all appear together on the last day. If supervisors are used for key characters you will need to appoint other adults to look after their factory units while they are up front.

Supervisors
These are the leaders of the units. Supervisors sit with the children in their units, relate closely to them and participate in the programme with them. They will also be involved in leading some games and activities. They, too, should be dressed in factory-style clothing, eg dungarees, overalls, boiler suits, etc.

Factory workers
These are the children, and they are placed in factory units of ten to twelve children, grouped according to age: eg 5–7s, 7–11s, 11–14s.

Band
The band is responsible for music but do not necessarily lead the singing. They should have a special name such as 'Bright Sparks'. Avoid making the music too complicated but keep it fairly up-tempo (electric keyboards, bass and electric guitar are ideal). A cassette (see Resources page) has been produced to help here, especially where churches may have difficulty finding musicians. A full band may not be needed if the LIGHT FACTORY cassette is used.

Chief engineer
This person looks after the sound, lights, projector and any other equipment needed.

PROGRAMME PREPARATION

It is best to begin preparation for any holiday club at least nine months prior to the event. For detailed advice on preparation, including appointing a leadership team, finance, publicity, follow-up, etc, see *Know How to Run a Holiday Club*, by David Savage, published by Scripture Union.

When the holiday club begins you will need to meet each day as a team for Bible study and prayer and to prepare the day's programme. Notes for team Bible study and prayer are provided in this material with each day's programme outline. Team Bible study and preparation for Day 1 will need to take place *before* the first day. Below are suggested daily timetables for a holiday club and for a club run during term time.

SUGGESTED DAILY TIMETABLES

Holiday club

9.15 – 9.30	Team members arrive
9.30 – 10.00	Team prayer and final preparations
10.00 – 10.15	Children arrive
10.15 – 12.00	Children go to units Programme takes place
12.00 – 12.30	Children leave Clear up
12.30 – 1.45	A very simple team lunch Evaluation Bible study and prayer for next day Team briefing and planning of next day
1.45 – 2.15	Preparation for next day
2.15	Team members leave

Term time club

6.15 – 6.30pm	Team members arrive
6.30 – 7.00	Team prayer and final preparations
7.00 – 8.30	Children go to units Programme takes place
8.30 – 8.45	Children leave Clear up
8.45 – 9.30	Evaluation Team prayer Team briefing and planning for next day Preparation for next day
9.30	Team members leave

As the term time club programme is fifteen minutes shorter than the holiday club programme, some items will need to be shortened or cut out. It is suggested that Assembly Line, twenty minutes of craft, games or activities, be left out and other items shortened. There is also less time for Bible study and preparation and it is suggested the team Bible study notes are used for personal daily devotions and referred to during the team prayer time at 6.30pm.

PROGRAMME ELEMENTS

Registration

As children arrive they should be registered. Information recorded should include the name of parent(s) or guardian(s), address, telephone number, age, school, church attended (if any), factory unit number. Depending on the number of churches involved in the holiday club, you may wish to record the name of any friend with whom a child comes. You are then able to direct him to the church of his friend at the end of the week. It is wise to record any allergies, recurring illness, or handicap. You will need to record each day which children are in attendance in case of fire or some other emergency. One way you may like to do this is by creating a clocking-in system where each child has a card with their name on display. They collect the card as they enter, have a date stamped on it and drop it in a 'clocking-in' box before going to their unit.

Time-and-a-half

This is the discussion, in units, of the overtime sheet (see below) received at the end of the previous day. This takes place informally as children arrive and go to their units and helps workers and supervisors get to know each other.

Walk-ons

Brief appearances made by key character(s) at various points of the programme. These should introduce the character and build an atmosphere of anticipation and mystery relating to the biblical teaching. Suggestions for what the key character(s) does on his/her walk-ons are given in each day's programme details.

Laser challenge

Children are given an opportunity to volunteer for a challenge up front. This is normally limited to three to six children each day. Children who wish to be involved enter at the beginning of the week by writing their names on individual slips of paper which are collected and kept in the 'Challenge bin' from which they are drawn each day. Each day any new children will need to be given the opportunity to enter. Children may only participate once in the week, so giving more the opportunity to take the challenge.

REGISTRATION FORM

Surname ______ First Name ______

Age: ___ years ___ months Date of Birth ______ Male/Female

Home Address ______

______

Telephone No. ______

Name of Parent(s)/Guardian(s) ______

School ______

Church ______

Friend with whom you came ______

Details of allergies, health, problems, handicaps

Unit No. ______

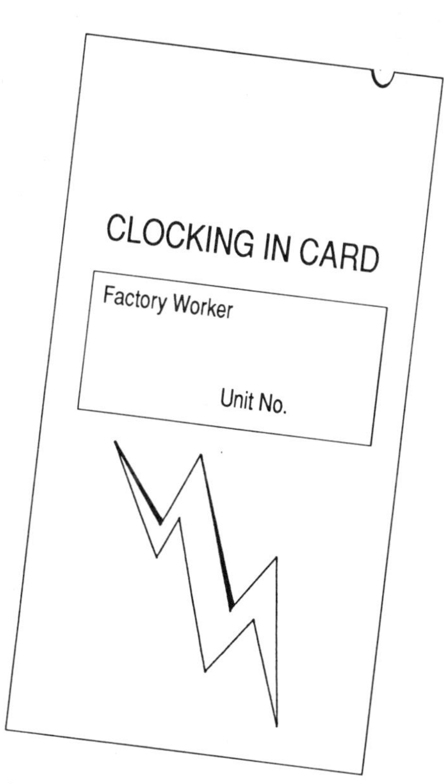

Most challenges are messy, so children should wear something to protect their clothing, such as bin liners with arm and head holes, and the floor should be covered so that any mess can be cleared up easily. The first *Laser challenge*, on Day 1, should be done with supervisors so children get some idea of what is involved. Children (and supervisors – Day 1) who take part should be given the 'I survived the *Laser challenge*' badge at the end.

Workout
Keep-fit exercises with a factory theme. You can create movements for the following exercises: scrub the floor, pull the lever, pack the box, load the lorry, etc. This should be done with lively music playing in the background.

Get-lit-go!
A fun activity explained at the beginning of each session. On a given signal units have to perform the task described as quickly as possible. The signal could be a flashing light, hooter, siren, etc.

Race through space
A mass quiz for all age groups. (See the quiz board layout.) You will need questions that vary in difficulty and are appropriate for the various age groups. Specific questions can then be directed at relevant factory units. Questions may be drawn from the biblical material, drama serial, etc. There should be some general knowledge questions for children unfamiliar with the Bible or who have come for the first time.

Spotlight
This section of the daily programme contains the main Bible teaching. It consists of finding out about the key Bible character through:
1. An interview with the key character – this introduces the key character and helps tell the Bible story.
2. Discussion in factory units – constructed so that it brings out the main point of the Bible story in a way appropriate to a particular age group.
3. Brief comments by presenters – who summarise the main points brought out in the interview and discussion.

Suggestions for these three elements are found at the end of each day's programme details.

Assembly line
Games, crafts or activities in age groups. Suggestions for these can be found at the back of this book. This is also an ideal time to serve refreshments.

T-break
The drama serial. Scripts are provided in this book.

Newsflash
Notices.

Overtime
An activity leaflet consisting of questions, puzzles, etc. They should be distributed at the end of each day for the children to complete at home, and then be discussed on the following day during *Time-and-a-half*. They are designed to help apply the day's teaching to the life of the child. They will also help the supervisors get to know the children in order to be more aware of individual needs which may become apparent. The *Overtime* sheets are found at the end of each day's programme details. You may like to photocopy the leaflets for the various age groups onto different-coloured paper.

LIP service
Lightning Independent Postal service. A post box should be put somewhere prominent so that the children can write to supervisors, presenters, or other workers as a way of asking questions and making comments.

Light Factory Song

Light Factory Light,
Sh-sh-sh-sh-shining bright.
All through the night,
Light Factory Light.
Come in and see,
You too can be,
In the Light Factory Light.

When your lights are going dim,
When you've blown a fuse,
Come into the Factory,
We'll show you what to do.

Let the light shine in you,
In the day and night.
Then you'll know the truth,
That Jesus is the Light.

Light Factory Light,
Sh-sh-sh-sh-shining bright.
All through the night,
Light Factory Light.
Come in and see,
You too can be,
In the Light Factory Light.

Shine, shine, shine, shine,
Shine, shine, shine, shine, shine,
 shine, shine, shine
 (double speed)
Sh-sh-sh-sh-sh-sh-sh-sh-sh-sh-sh-
 sh-sh-sh-shine.

Light Factory Light,
Sh-sh-sh-sh-shining bright.
All through the night,
Light Factory Light.
Come in and see,
You too can be,
In the Light Factory Light.

Come in and see,
You too can be,
In the Light Factory Light.
Factory Light. (getting quieter)
Factory Light.
Factory Light. (whisper)
FACTORY LIGHT! (shout)

The actions

Light Factory Light
(Punch the air dramatically to emphasise the movements. Hold the arms out in front of the body, elbows bent, and slice the air with the forearms and hands.)

Sh -sh -sh -sh shining bright
(Rotate hands round each other and then stretch out.)

All through the night
(Right then left, hands covering eyes and then down by sides.)

Light Factory Light
(As before.)

Come in and see
(Right then left hands bent with thumbs pointing behind.)

You too can be
(Right then left, arms out to side with thumbs pointing at neighbour.)

In the Light Factory Light
(As before.)

(NB 'Let the light shine in you . . .' – clap hands above head.)

Light Fact'ry Light

Words and music by
Janet Morgan, Andy Paine and Sue Radford

G

Light light light light light light light light

light light light light light light light light

Light fac - t'ry light sh - sh - sh sh-shin - ing bright

C G

All through the night Light fac - t'ry light

D7 C G

Come on and see you too can be in the light fac - t'ry light

2nd time, go to *

♩ = ♪

F C F C

When your light is go-ing dim If you've blown a fuse

F C

♪ = ♩

A7 D7

come in to the fac - to-ry We'll show you what to do! Yeah!

G C D7 G
Let the Light shine in you In the day and night
C D G
Then you'll know the truth that Je - sus is the Light
*G
Shine, shine, shine, shine,
shine, shine, shine, shine, shine, shine, shine, shine, sh - sh - sh - sh - sh - sh - sh - sh -
- sh - sh - sh - sh - sh - sh-SHINE Light fac - t'ry light
sh - sh - sh - sh - shin - ing bright All through the night
Light fac - t'ry light
Come on and see
you too can be in the light fac - t'ry light
1st time
D.𝄋
2nd time
fac - t'ry light
fac - t'ry light fac - t'ry light Fac - t'ry Light! Yeah!

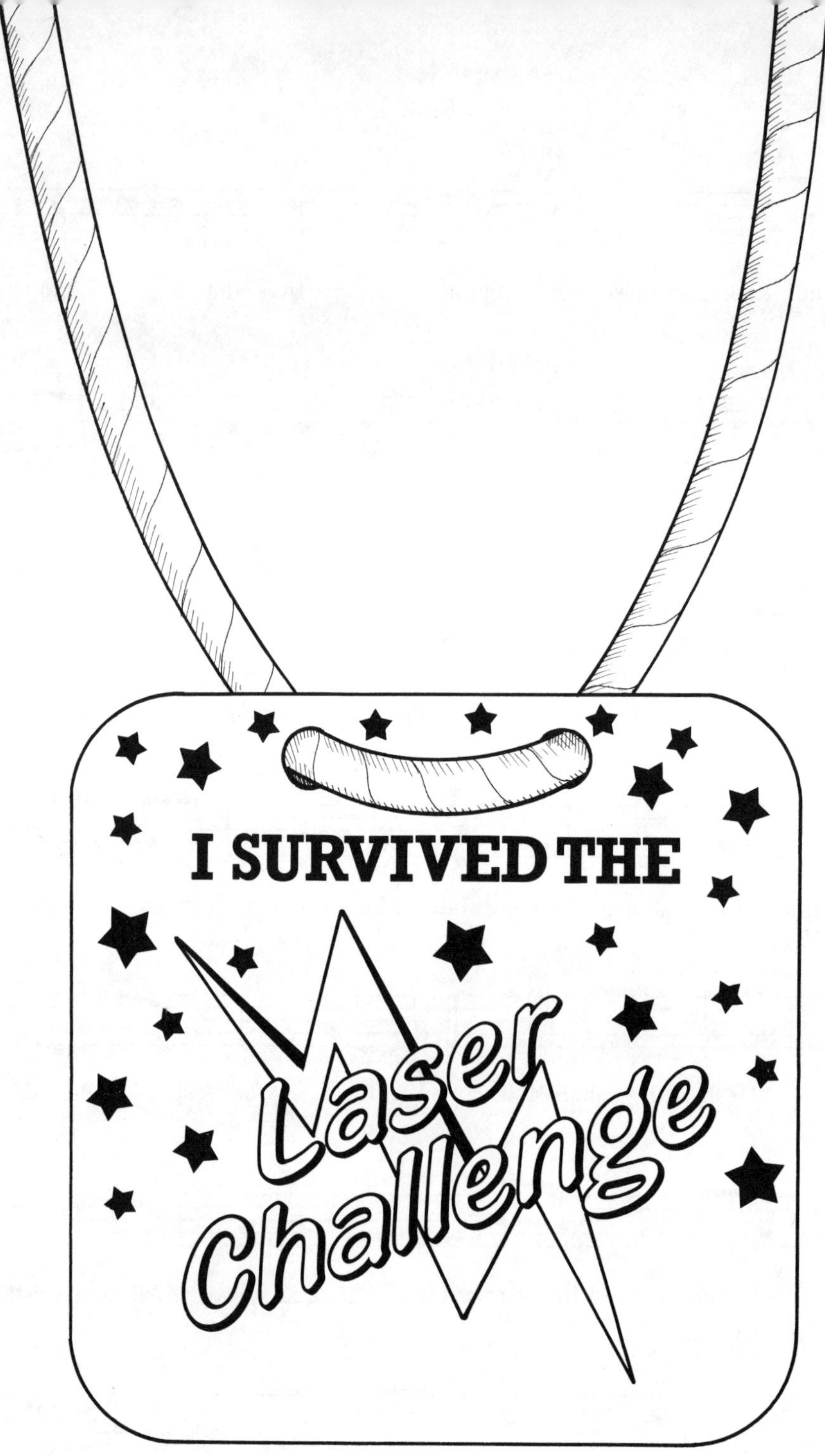

Laser challenge badge

Photocopy this onto coloured paper and stick it onto firm card. Colour the logo in.

Either attach a safety pin to the back of the badge or loop a piece of coloured string or cloth through the holes.

Photocopy this diagram or use it as a guide to produce your own hats on card. Enlarge to 13" high by 11.25" wide.
To make the hat cut out shape: the children may colour in or produce their own designs. Cut along the slits and be careful not to cut beyond the lines.Bring the ends together and fit into one of the slots.

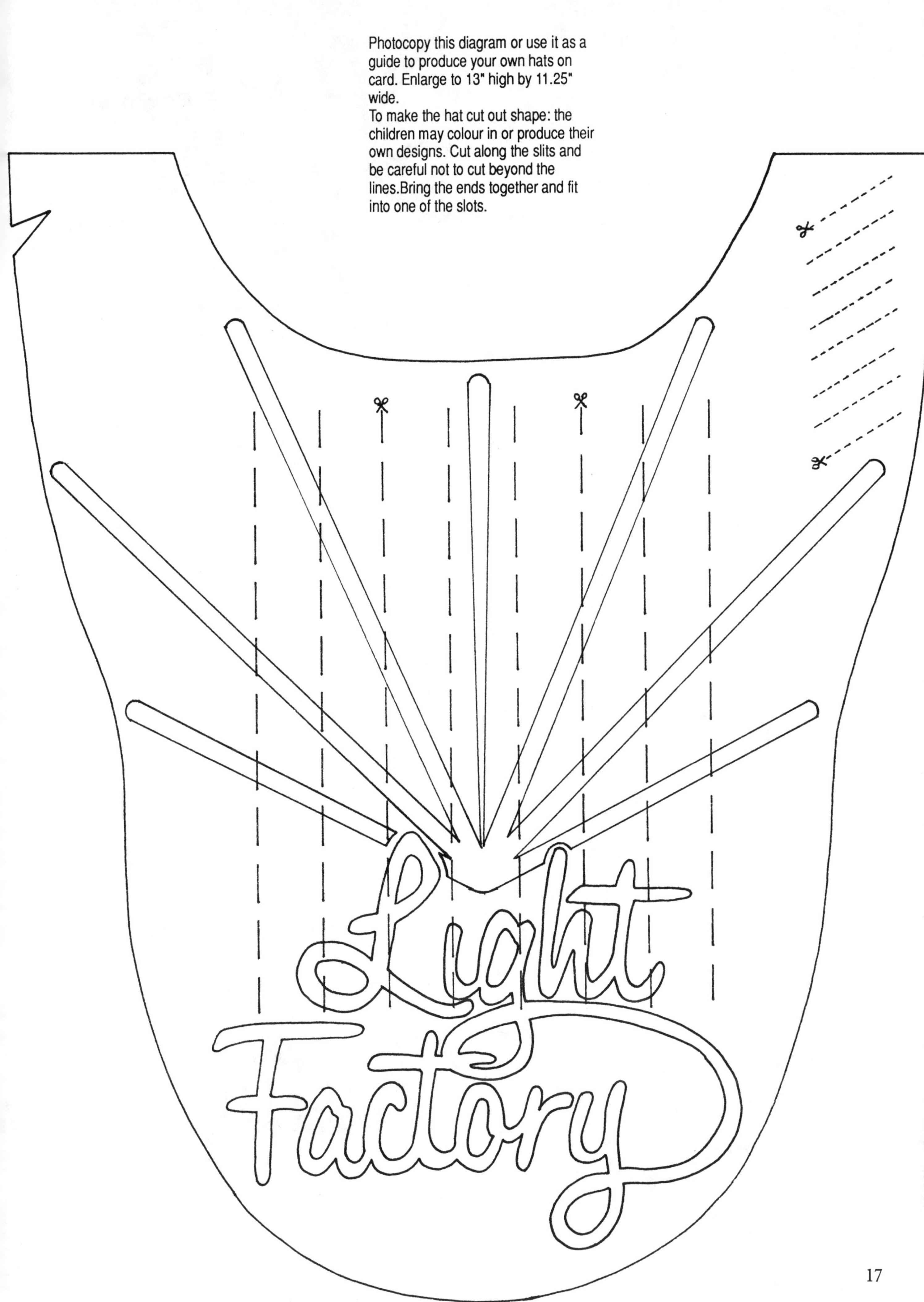

Light
Factory

The Light of the world

John the Baptist proclaims who Jesus is

Bible material
John 1:1–34

Key character
John the Baptist

Key verse
John 8:12. (The key verse each day is not necessarily intended for use as a memory verse for children; on some days it is suitable only for use with leaders.)

Key aim
To introduce Jesus – the Light of the world – as seen through the message of John the Baptist.

TEAM BIBLE STUDY AND PRAYER

Pray
Ask God to help you to understand more of what it means to say that Jesus is the Light of the world.

Read
John 1:1–28

John the Baptist was the last of the 'Old Testament' prophets. His preaching was powerful and he drew many followers. His appearance was striking – he reminded people of descriptions of Elijah – and his diet was very interesting! The preaching of this man, who dressed in animal skins and ate locusts and honey, was having a tremendous influence on people's lives. Many of them were turning from the wrong things they did and making a new start. As a sign of the sincerity of their repentance, people came to John to be baptised by him in the local rivers. There is no doubt about it – John caused a lot of interest, yet no-one was entirely sure who he was. Instead of introducing himself, he spent time explaining exactly who he *wasn't*!

Discuss
Who did John claim *not* to be?

Read
John 1:29–34

In contrast, Jesus was about to begin his ministry. He was a thirty-year-old carpenter. We do not read that he was anything other than of ordinary appearance and ate the usual Jewish food. Yet the very 'charismatic' John the Baptist proclaimed this seemingly ordinary Jesus to be the one that everyone had been waiting for.

Discuss
Who did John say that Jesus was?

Reflect
John had the same role as we have in this first LIGHT FACTORY session. This is described succinctly in John 1:6–9. John was not the light, he came to tell people who the 'real light' was – Jesus. This is exactly what we wish to do in our first visit to the LIGHT FACTORY.

Pray
Focus your attention on some element of light in the room and think about its function eg. a lamp, a fire, a ray of sunshine. Now read John 8:12 quietly to yourself several times. Think about what it means for Jesus to be the Light of *your* world! Now ask God to make those thoughts reality in your experience today.

PROGRAMME AT A GLANCE

Time	Activity
10.00	Registration
10.35	LIGHT FACTORY song
10.38	Welcome/introduction
10.41	Teach LIGHT FACTORY song
10.49	Walk-on 1
10.51	Laser challenge
10.59	Walk-on 2
11.00	Workout
11.03	Spotlight interview
11.06	Discussion in units
11.21	Closing comments
11.25	Song(s)
11.28	T-break
11.35	Assembly line
11.55	Overtime
11.56	Newsflash
11.57	LIGHT FACTORY song
12.00	Finish

WHAT YOU WILL NEED

Registration

- Registration cards, clocking-in cards
- clocking-in box
- date stamp

Stage area

- LIGHT FACTORY cassette and/or music for songs
- Words to songs on overhead transparencies or large card
- Music cassette for *workout* (aerobics)
- Bible character: John the Baptist costume and props
- *Laser challenge: Laser challenge* bin, *Laser challenge* badges, bin liners, floor covering; three bowls of honey with six pieces of carrot in each, three plates of flour, three frying pans
- *Spotlight* interview questions and notes for comment
- Notices
- LIP service post box
- Drama serial: broom, duster, table

Units

- Programme at a glance
- Bible
- *Spotlight* discussion questions
- *Overtime* sheets
- Entry forms for *Laser challenge*
- Hats
- Felt pens or crayons and scissors for making hats

Age groups

- Equipment and materials for activities
- Games and crafts in age groups

Programme details

10.00
Registration
You may like to begin registering children at 10.00am on the first day. They can then go straight to their units where they will meet their supervisors and make their factory hats. A pattern for the hat will need to be printed on card as they need to last the entire week. You will need to ensure that the children write their names on their hats. They should leave their hats with their supervisors at the end of each day.

10.35
LIGHT FACTORY song
Presenters sing the LIGHT FACTORY song and do the actions.

10.38
Welcome and introductions
Presenters welcome everyone to the LIGHT FACTORY and then introduce themselves, the band, the foremen, and acknowledge the supervisors by asking them to stand, and the workers (children) likewise. This should be done in a lively way.

10.41
Teach LIGHT FACTORY song
Teach the theme song to the workers.

10.49
Walk-on 1
John the Baptist walks across the stage in biblical dress, carrying a jar of honey, shouting, 'Repent! Turn away from your sins and be baptised and God will forgive your sins!' Presenters look baffled and carry on with the programme.

10.51
Laser challenge
Only leaders should be involved in this the first day. Three supervisors should be chosen before the programme to take part in it. They are called forward to the stage area and asked to sit at a table facing the workers. A bowl of honey with 6 'locusts' in it (bits of carrot), a plateful of flour and a frying pan are placed in front of each supervisor. As quickly as possible, with hands behind their backs and using only their mouths, they must retrieve each locust from their bowl of honey, dip the locust in flour and place them in the frying pan. At the finish they all receive *Laser challenge* badges for taking part.

Presenters explain to the workers that there will be a different *Laser challenge* each day and that they will be given the opportunity to enter their names if they wish to. Names will be drawn from the *Challenge* bin each day.

10.59
Walk-on 2
As before, shouting, 'I am the voice of someone shouting in the desert: make a straight path for the Lord to travel!'

11.00
Workout
Factory keep-fit

11.03
Spotlight
Interview (11.03) John the Baptist walks on again shouting, 'This is the one I was talking about. He comes after me, but he is greater than I am.' The presenter stops him this time and proceeds with the interview.

Main points to bring out. Ensure that the interview brings out the point that John recognised Jesus as being the Light of the world and was prepared to proclaim it to everyone – including the children in the LIGHT FACTORY. After John has been interrupted in mid-sentence, the presenters should begin to ask him questions about who he is and what he's doing there. John could reply by saying who he is *not*, as he did in John 1:19–23. In the conversation, John should bring out that he is not the Light of the world but that he has come to tell others who *is* – Jesus. John should finish by explaining that the Light of the world has arrived. The presenter could take the opportunity to mention that we will be meeting some other people who also recognised Jesus as being the Light of the world. We will have the opportunity to learn more about him in the LIGHT FACTORY.

Interview questions. Use these questions as a basis to give John the opportunity to develop the main point:

- Who are you?
- What are you doing?
- Where have you come from?
- Why are you dressed like that?
- What are you eating?
- Why are you telling people about Jesus?
- Does anyone believe you?

Discussion in units (11.06). Workers are given the opportunity to enter their names for the *Laser challenge.*

Discussion questions

5–7s

- Have you ever heard of Jesus before?
- What sort of things did Jesus do or say?
- Who first told you about Jesus?

7–11s

- Have you ever heard of Jesus before?
- Who do you think Jesus is?
- Who first told you about Jesus?

Spotlight comment (11.21). Presenter draws the attention of the units to the front and gives closing comments.

The presenter should take the opportunity to summarise today's learning and firmly establish that Jesus is the Light of the world. Begin by acknowledging that the children are at different stages of their understanding about who Jesus is. The *spotlight* comment could be something similar to this:

'Some of you know lots about Jesus, others of you don't know very much yet. Jesus was called the "Light of the world" for a very special reason. Just as light shows up everything that is in the darkness so Jesus brought light and sunshine to people's lives by loving them, caring for them, teaching and healing them. The light also shows up things that are wrong and Jesus did the same because he was perfect. We are going to meet people like John the Baptist who discovered how Jesus could be the Light of the world in their lives and be their friend. Jesus was just so amazing that when people met him it was as if all the lights in the world had come on!

If it seems appropriate, say a short prayer.

11.25
Song(s)
Choose from the cassette, or choose songs with which the children are familiar.

11.28
T-break
Drama serial, episode 1

11.35
Assembly line
Games, crafts or activities in age groups. (See the suggestions given at the back of this book.) At the end of *Assembly line,* workers come back together in units.

11.55
Overtime
Presenters introduce the *Overtime* sheet which is to be completed at home and brought back the following morning. The workers collect these from their supervisors.

11.56
Newsflash
Notices. The workers will need to be reminded to leave their hats with their supervisors and encouraged to bring friends along tomorrow. This is also a good time to announce any family events and remind them of the 10.15 starting time tomorrow.

11.57
LIGHT FACTORY song

12.00
Finish

Write your name in the box.

John's best food was honey.
What is your best food?

John wore a hairy coat and leather belt.
What do you wear?

John's special friend was Jesus.
Who is your special friend?

Can you find these lights in the picture below?

Light bulb
Lamp
Torch
Candle
Traffic lights

Put a circle around each of them.

John told people about the Light of the world. Join these dots to find out who this is.

Jesus

John told people about the Light. Shade in the spaces marked with a •
to find out who this is.

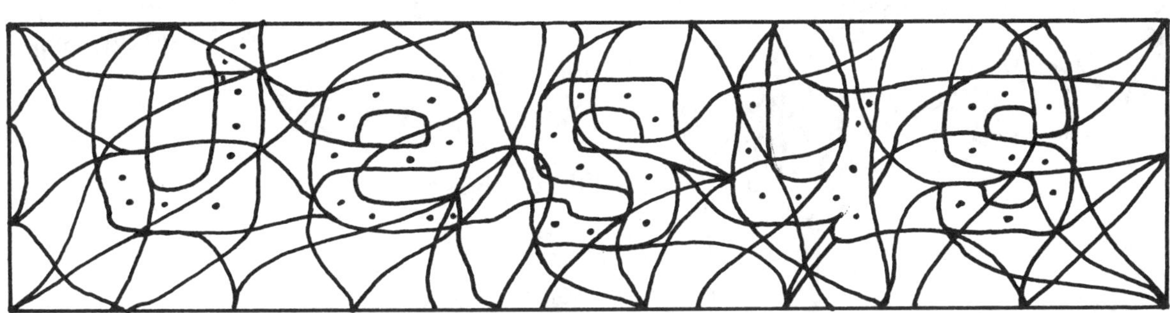

Light Fax

My favourite:

Food

TV programme

Lesson at school

In the space below write the names and ages of everyone in your family who lives in the same house as you.

SOLVE THE RIDDLE

My first is in tea but not in coffee
My second is in chocolate and also in toffee
My third is in brown and also in green
My fourth is in lurch but never in lean
My fifth is in touch and also in sight
My whole is useful for giving out light

What am I?

(Answer at bottom of page)

We got to know a little about John the Baptist today. What do you think he would say was his:

favourite food?

favourite clothes?

most special person?

WRITE DOWN YOUR FAVOURITE:

food

TV programme

singer or group

clothes

sport

person

JESUS – THE LIGHT OF THE WORLD

What kind of light best describes Jesus for you?

(Answer: Torch)

An encounter with the Light

A Samaritan woman finds that Jesus knows all about her

Bible material
John 4:1–42

Key character
Samaritan woman

Key verses
Psalm 139:1–6

Key aim
To present Jesus – the Light of the world – as the one who knows everything about us, as illustrated by his encounter with the Samaritan woman.

TEAM BIBLE STUDY AND PRAYER

Pray
Spend a few minutes opening yourself up to God and telling him the things on your mind. Remember, he made you and he knows you through and through.

Read
John 4:1–15

The Samaritan woman was not only very surprised that Jesus asked her for water, she was amazed that he had spoken to her at all. A Jewish man would never be seen speaking to a woman in public – not even to his wife or daughter. Jewish men regularly thanked God that they were not women! That Jesus chose to speak to this woman would therefore have been surprising enough, but then to discover that the woman was a Samaritan would really have sent the shock waves through Jewish society. The Samaritans and Jews had been on bad terms for many years. The original disagreement was about the correct place for worship. The Jews said it was the Temple in Jerusalem while the Samaritans insisted it was on Mount Gerizim. Like many situations of this nature, the original disagreement lay firmly in history but the prejudice continued.

Discuss
What is my attitude towards the other Supervisors and the children in my factory unit? Am I like a traditional Jewish man – full of pride and prejudice – or am I like Jesus, willing to make the first move across boundaries of fear and prejudice?

Read
John 4:16–42

Jesus knew this woman through and through. He understood her background, he knew her personal history and he responded to her need for 'living water'. He was light in her dark places.

Discuss
Do you think that the woman felt threatened or relieved by Jesus' knowledge of her? (Read John 4:16–19, 28–30.)

Reflect
Jesus – the Light of the world – knows us just as he knew the Samaritan woman. He knows our background, our personal histories and our needs. He also knows the children in our factory units through and through and wants to bring light into their dark places. This is what we wish to communicate on our second visit to the LIGHT FACTORY.

Pray
Thank God that he knows you through and through. Read Psalm 139:1–6 aloud – saying the words to God.

PROGRAMME AT A GLANCE

Time	Activity
10.00	Registration
10.15	Time-and-a-half
10.30	LIGHT FACTORY song
10.33	Welcome
10.36	Get-lit-go! explanation
10.39	Walk-on 1
10.40	T-break
10.47	Laser challenge
10.55	Walk-on 2
10.56	Workout
10.59	Get-lit-go!
11.02	Song(s)
11.07	Spotlight interview
11.11	Discussion in units
11.23	Comment
11.26	Assembly line
11.46	LIP service explanation
11.49	Get-lit-go!
11.52	Newsflash/overtime
11.57	LIGHT FACTORY song
12.00	Finish

WHAT YOU WILL NEED

Registration
- Registration cards
- clocking-in cards
- clocking-in box
- date stamp

Stage area
- LIGHT FACTORY cassette and/or music for songs
- Words to songs on overhead transparencies or large card
- Music cassette for *workout* (aerobics)
- Bible character: costume for Samaritan woman; water jug
- *Laser challenge: Laser challenge bin, Laser challenge* badges, bin liners, floor covering; plastic cups with water, three trays, squares of stiff card
- *Spotlight* interview questions and notes for comment
- Notices
- LIP service post box
- Drama serial: walkie-talkie radio

Units
- Programme at a glance
- Bible
- *Get-lit-go!* Bin liner for each unit
- *Spotlight* discussion questions
- *Overtime* sheets
- Entry forms for *Laser challenge*
- Hats
- Felt pens or crayons and scissors for making hats

Age groups
- Equipment and materials for activities
- Games and crafts in age groups

Programme details

10.00
Registration
Register any new children and place them in a factory unit.

10.15
Time-and-a-half
Welcome any new workers into your units and give them factory hats to make. Discuss *Overtime* sheets with workers who took them home the previous day. (Have extras for those who may have left them at home.)

10.30
LIGHT FACTORY song

10.33
Welcome
Presenters welcome the workers and draw special attention to any new workers. Using the clock face give a quick run-down of the exciting things happening in the LIGHT FACTORY today.

10.36
Get-lit-go! explanation
(This is only the explanation. Units are not to do the Get-Lit-Go! at this point.) Presenters explain to the workers that at a given signal (demonstrate the signal) they must, in their units, take their shoes off and place them in a bin liner held by their supervisor. The supervisor will then shake them up and from the bag give every worker two shoes to put on. As each unit completes this task, they should cheer loudly so presenters can see who is finished. Explain that the signal will come unexpectedly at any time in the programme and they must act quickly when they hear it.

10.39
Walk-on 1
The Samaritan woman, dressed in biblical clothes, walks across the stage area with a water pot on her head or shoulder. Presenters look bemused.

10.40
T-break
Drama serial, episode 2. Presenters announce it is time for *T-break* and Glad enters.

10.47
Laser challenge
Presenters announce that it is time for *Laser challenge.* The names of six workers are drawn from the *Challenge bin* and those six workers are asked to come to the stage area. They are to work in pairs with one lying on his/her back with a tray resting on his/her stomach. Their partners must stack as many cups of water as possible on the tray until they topple over. The cups of water are stacked by placing first a cup of water then a piece of stiff card on top of the cup, another cup of water then another card, etc. Cups should be prepared beforehand and contain not more than ¾″ water. Have towels ready for workers to dry themselves. Present the *Laser challenge* badges to the participants when finished.

10.55
Walk-on 2
As before. Says to the audience, 'Come and see the man who told me everything I ever did!' Walks off.

10.56
Workout
Factory keep-fit.

10.59
Get-lit-go!
The signal goes without warning. Presenters should comment throughout, encouraging the workers on. Give time at the end for all workers to retrieve their own shoes.

11.02
Song(s)
Choose from the cassette, or other songs with which the workers are familiar.

11.07
Spotlight
Interview (11.07) Woman walks on again saying, 'He told me everything I ever did,' but this time the presenters stop her and proceed with interview.

Main points to bring out. Ensure that the interview brings out that Jesus knew the Samaritan woman better than anyone else.

Try to make the story unfold. Question her about why she was at the well, where she came from and who she met there. Ensure that the woman brings out that the most amazing aspect of her meeting with Jesus was that he knew all about her home, her family and her lifestyle. Try also to bring out some of the background information: she would have been surprised that a Jewish man would speak to her, a woman; also, it was amazing that Jesus should speak to anyone who was a Samaritan.

Interview questions. Use these questions as a basis to give the Samaritan woman the opportunity to develop the main point:

- Why were you at the well?
- Who did you meet there?
- What happened?
- Why was that surprising?
- What was special about this person?

Discussion in units (11.11). Workers are given the opportunity to enter their names for the *Laser challenge*.

Discussion questions

5–7s
- Was the Samaritan woman surprised that Jesus knew all about her?
- Who knows you best?
- Do they know what you do?
- Do they see everything you do?
- Does anybody know what you are thinking about?
- Is there anybody who can?

7–11s
- Was the Samaritan woman surprised that Jesus knew all about her?
- Who knows you best?
- Do you ever have secrets that not even that person knows?
- Would you ever share them with anyone?
- Do you ever talk to God about them?
- Why?

11–14s
- Who knows you best?
- How much do they know about you?
- If someone knows lots about you, do you find it frightening or reassuring?
- What makes the difference as to how you feel about someone knowing you well?

Spotlight comment (11.23). The presenter draws the attention of the units to the front and gives closing comments.

The presenter should take this opportunity to summarise today's learning and develop the idea that the Light of the world shone into the woman's life and revealed everything about her. It is important to emphasise the positive aspect of Jesus really knowing us. The intention is not to give the children the impression that Jesus turns the spotlight only on all the wrong things they've done that no one else knows! The idea is to communicate that Jesus knows *and cares about* everything in our lives.

Begin by reading out Psalm 139:1–6 from a modern version of the Bible, such as the *Good News* version. There is no need to give the actual reference, simply say that those words came from the Bible. Follow this with a very simple comment such as 'just as Jesus knew all about the Samaritan woman, he knows all about you and me!'

11.26
Assembly line
Games, crafts or activities in age groups. At the end of *Assembly line*, workers come back together in their units.

11.46
LIP service explanation
Presenters introduce workers to the Lightning Independent Postal Service. Encourage them to write to LIP service with their comments and questions.

11.49
Get-lit-go!
Repeat the above.

11.52
Newsflash/overtime
Notices. Remind the workers to leave their hats with their supervisors, bring friends, etc. Tell them to collect their *Overtime* sheets from their supervisors and bring them back tomorrow.

11.57
LIGHT FACTORY song

12.00
Finish

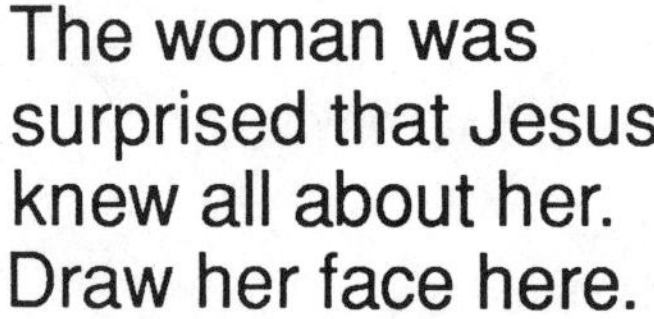

The woman was surprised that Jesus knew all about her. Draw her face here.

JESUS KNOWS ALL ABOUT YOU TOO

DRAW YOURSELF HERE

Jesus knows when we are happy and sad

What makes you happy?

....

What things make you sad?

....

My name is ....

Colour in the shapes below to find out what the Samaritan woman told her friend about Jesus.

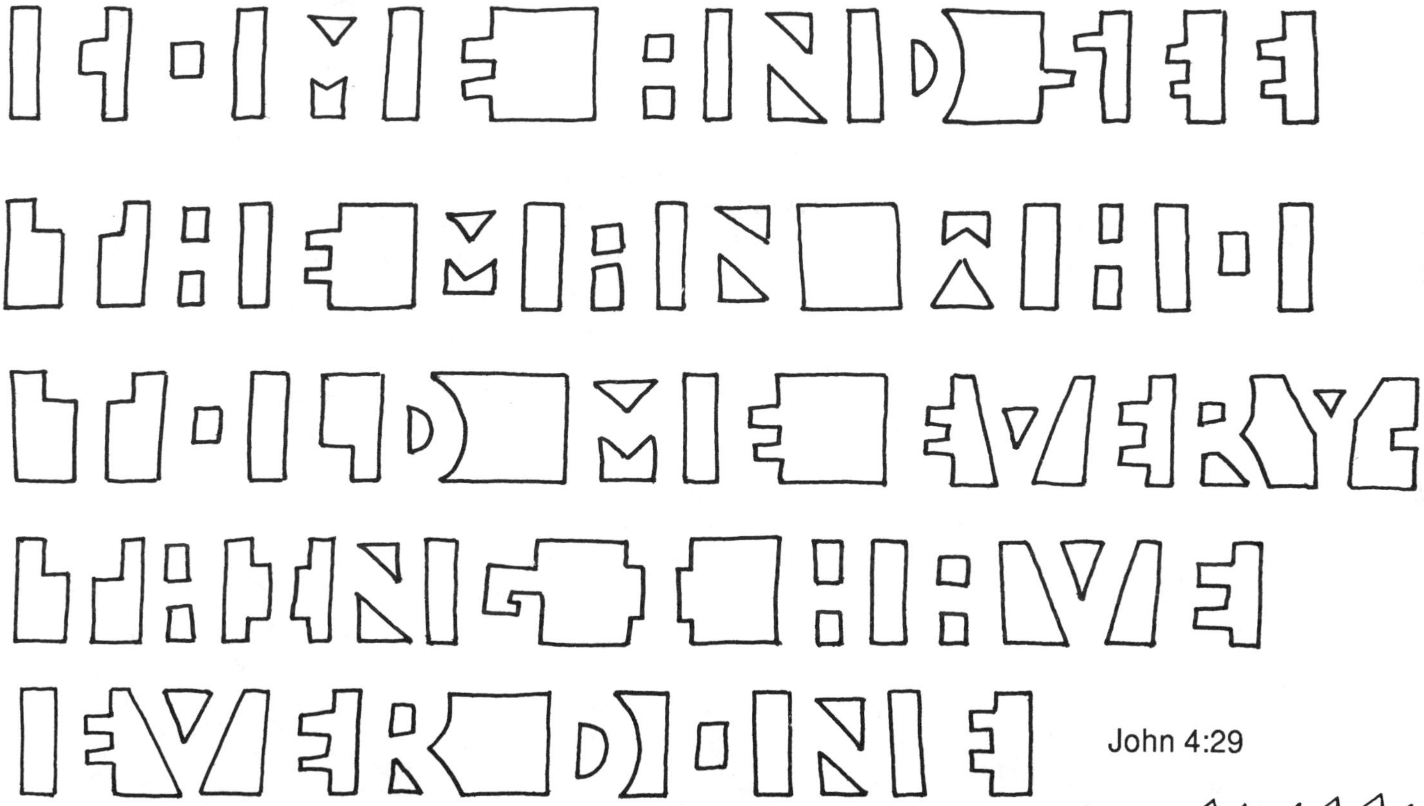

John 4:29

Light Fax

Happy sad worried

puzzled scared

The Bible tells us that God knows everything about us, too. Here are some of the things it says. Draw the face that best shows how you feel about these things

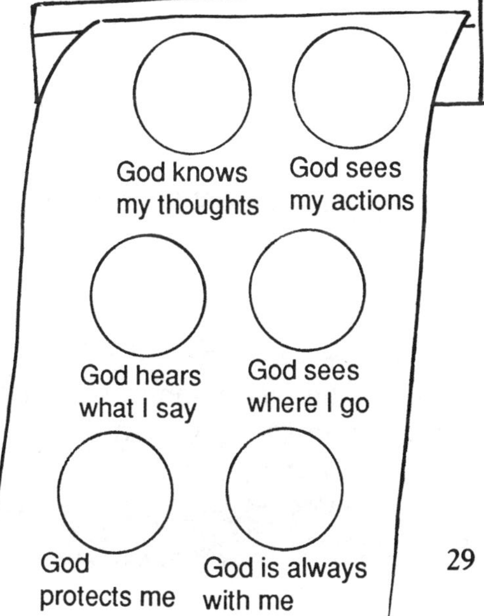

Yes you! write your name in the space.

We have loads of different images, depending on where we are:

COOL SKOOL

LOCAL SAINT

TRENDY WENDY

HOME COMFORTS

...But there's a real you trying to get out. Fill in the inside-out fact file.

FACT FILE

The real (full name)

....

My best point

....

My worst point

....

My strongest feeling

....

My biggest dream for the future

....

My greatest fear

....

My greatest hope

....

The person I most care about

....

If you want to keep some of this private, don't write it down. Do talk to someone you trust, instead, if you want to.

God knows the real you. In fact, he probably knows you better than you know yourself. Read these verses from Psalm 139 and fill in the blank faces next to each one with the expression that best reflects your feelings.

happy

sad · bored

worried

angry

puzzled · scared

(You can use any face more than once.)

Lord, you have examined me and you know me

You see me whether I am working or resting; you know all my actions.

You are all around me on every side; you protect me with your power.

You know everything I do; from far away you understand all my thoughts.

Even before I speak, you already know what I will say.

Your knowledge of me is too deep; it is beyond my understanding.

Where could I go to escape from you? Where could I get away from your presence? If I went up to heaven, you would be there, If I lay down in the world of the dead, you would be there.

A conversation with the Light

Jesus listens to and talks with Mary and Martha at Lazarus' tomb

Bible material
John 11:1–44

Key characters
Mary, Martha, Lazarus

Key verse
Psalm 119:105

Key aim
To present Jesus – the Light of the world – as one who listens and speaks to us, as illustrated by his conversation with Mary and Martha at Lazarus' tomb.

TEAM BIBLE STUDY AND PRAYER

Pray
Ask God to speak to you and to help you to *listen* to what he is saying.

Read
John 11:1–17

Mary and Martha were disappointed with Jesus. He had spent a great deal of time in their home, they had been generous with their hospitality and they thought of him as a close friend. Where was he when they needed him? They sent a message but he chose not to come immediately. In the intervening period their brother, Lazarus – Jesus' friend – had died.

Discuss
How did each of the central characters in the story feel? Think of a word to describe Mary's feelings, Martha's feelings and Jesus' feelings before the raising of Lazarus.

Read
John 11:18–44

Jesus did not apologise for his late arrival and then tell Lazarus to come out of the tomb! Most of the chapter concentrates on Jesus' conversations with Mary and Martha after his arrival. Jesus took time to listen to Martha's complaint about his lateness, he took hers and Mary's feelings into account. They would have known how well he understood what they were saying because he showed how he felt about Lazarus' death. Finally he spent time talking and explaining deeper truths to them. He listened, he understood, he talked with them. He knew how to be with grieving people and had the power to turn a funeral into a fantastic celebration and their sorrow into joy. While Jesus was around nothing was ever 'too late' and life was far from boring.

Discuss
Do I listen to the children in my factory unit? Am I like Jesus in my conversations with them and with the other Supervisors?

Reflect
Jesus still listens, understands and speaks to us today. We can talk to him about anything. He understands and speaks to us through his Spirit and his word, the Bible. His word is a light when we don't know what to do or where to go. It is very important that the children are listened to by us. It is also important that they realise they can talk to Jesus, that he will listen and he will speak to them. What he says to them will be light to them in this third visit to the LIGHT FACTORY.

Pray
Read John 11:41–42 again. Thank God that just as he listened to Jesus, he listens to us. Read Psalm 119:105. Thank God that he continues to shed light on our lives through his word.

PROGRAMME AT A GLANCE

Time	Activity
10.15	Time-and-a-half
10.25	LIGHT FACTORY song
10.29	Welcome
10.31	Walk-on 1
10.32	Get-lit-go! explanation
10.35	Race through space
10.47	Walk-on 2
10.48	Get-lit-go!
10.51	Spotlight interview
10.55	Discussion
11.07	Comment
11.10	Workout
11.13	T-break
11.18	Laser challenge
11.26	LIP service
11.29	Song(s)
11.34	Assembly line
11.54	Newsflash/overtime
11.57	LIGHT FACTORY song
12.00	Finish

WHAT YOU WILL NEED

Registration
- Registration cards
- clocking-in cards
- clocking-in box
- date stamp

STAGE AREA
- LIGHT FACTORY cassette and/or music for songs
- Words to songs on overhead transparencies or large card
- Music cassette for *workout* (aerobics)
- Bible characters: biblical costumes for Mary and Martha and strips of white cloth to wrap around Lazarus
- *Laser challenge: Laser challenge* bin, *Laser challenge* badges, bin liners, floor covering; three protective goggles, shaving foam, three full water pistols
- *Spotlight* interview questions and notes for comment
- Notices
- LIP service post box
- *Race through space*: quiz board and questions

Units
- Programme at a glance
- Bible
- *Get-lit-go!* Several polo mints, and a drinking straw for every worker in each unit
- *Spotlight* discussion questions
- *Overtime* sheets
- Entry forms for *Laser challenge*
- Hats
- Felt pens or crayons and scissors for making hats

Age groups
- Equipment and materials for activities, games and crafts.

Programme details

10.15
Time-and-a-half
Welcome new workers. Discuss *Overtime* sheets.

10.25
LIGHT FACTORY song

10.29
Welcome
Welcome the workers and give a run-down of what's happening today.

10.31
Walk-on 1
Lazarus, in strips of white material resembling an Egyptian mummy, walks slowly across the stage area followed by an amazed Mary and Martha (in biblical dress).

10.32
Get-lit-go! Explanation
Explain to the workers that at the given signal, the workers must get into a straight line in their units. The supervisors will then give to every worker in their unit a drinking straw which they must place in their mouths. A Polo mint will then be placed on the drinking straw of the worker at the end of the queue who will then pass the Polo to the straw of next worker (without touching it with their hands) and so on to the end of the queue. A loud cheer is given by the units as they finish. Each supervisor should have a few spare Polos in case the first is dropped or broken.

10.35
Race through space
Presenters lead the workers in a quiz using the *Race through space* quiz board.

10.47
Walk-on 2
As before. This time Mary and Martha chatting happily, 'I just can't believe it!' 'Isn't it wonderful?' 'It's amazing!' etc.

10.48
Get-lit-go!
The supervisor should collect all the drinking straws from the workers at the end of Get-lit-go!

10.51
Spotlight
Interview. Lazarus, Mary and Martha walk on again and this time are stopped by the presenters and proceed with interview.

Main points to bring out. Ensure that the interview brings out the quality of the friendship between Jesus, Mary, Martha and Lazarus. Jesus listened to their problems, responded to them and shared how well he understood them.

Only Martha and Martha should be involved in the interview, with Lazarus standing in the background. The presenter should bring out the relationship that Mary and Martha had with Jesus and try to leave Lazarus until the very end. Establish the quality of the friendship by bringing out how natural it would be for Mary and Martha to want Jesus there when there was a problem in the family. Encourage Mary and Martha to talk about how they felt about the situation. Bring in Lazarus at the end by asking him how much he values Jesus' friendship.

Interview questions. Use these questions as a basis to give Mary, Martha and Lazarus the opportunity to develop the main point:
- Who are you?
- Where is your home?
- Who is this (referring to Lazarus)?
- What happened to him?
- What did you do when Lazarus died?
- Have you been friends with Jesus for long?
- What did Jesus do?
- Did you feel that Jesus understood how you felt?
- How do you feel about Jesus, Lazarus?

Discussion in units (10.55). Workers are given the opportunity to enter their names for the *Laser challenge*.

Discussion questions
5–7s
- Have you ever had a really good friend?
- What sort of things did you do together?
- What do you talk about with them?
- Was Jesus a good friend to Mary, Martha and Lazarus
- Why?
- How can we talk to Jesus?

7–11s

- Have you ever had a good friend?
- What makes a good friend?
- How did Jesus show he was a good friend?
- Does Jesus ever talk to you?

11–14s

- What qualities do you value in a good friend?
- Do you tell them everything?
- Do you ever feel lonely even when you're with other people?
- Do you ever talk to Jesus about things?
- How do you think he could talk to you?

Questions for everyone

- If Jesus were sitting next to you now, what would you say to him?

Spotlight comment (11.07). Presenter draws attention of the units to the front and gives closing comments

The presenter should take this opportunity to summarise today's learing and establish the fact that Jesus can be a good friend to the children in the LIGHT FACTORY just as he was to Mary, Martha and Lazarus.

Develop further the quality of the Jesus/Mary/Martha/Lazarus friendship. They were such good friends that they could spend time talking about anything. Whether they were happy or sad, relaxed or angry they could talk about it with Jesus. They were absolutely sure that he would listen to them, understand how they felt and always help. We can talk to Jesus, too, and know that he will listen, understand and help even if he doesn't always do what we think he ought to. Martha thought Jesus should have come quicker before Lazarus died. What she didn't know was that he was in control and knew he would raise Lazarus from the dead. He doesn't always do what we want him to, but he does do the best for us.

He not only listens, but he speaks to us – through the Bible, other people and the Holy Spirit. We can learn more about listening to him and we will as we spend more time in the LIGHT FACTORY. Let's talk to him now . . . (say a prayer).

11.10
Workout
Factory keep-fit

11.13
T-Break
Drama serial, episode 3

11.18
Laser challenge
Presenters draw the names of three workers out of the Challenge bin. Place a bin liner and protective goggles on each worker. Stand the workers in the stage area as if they were on the three corners of a triangle approximately ten feet apart and facing the centre. Put a large portion of shaving foam on the nose of each worker and give each worker a full water pistol. At a given signal they have one minute to see how much shaving foam they can squirt off each others' noses. (Have water and towels ready for the participants to wash their faces.) Present the *Laser challenge* badges to the three participants.

11.26
LIP service
Remind the workers about LIP service. Make any appropriate comments on any letters received.

11.29
Song(s)
Choose from the cassette or from songs with which the workers are familiar.

11.34
Assembly line
Games, crafts, or activities in age groups.

11.54
Newsflash/overtime
Notices. Remind the workers to leave their hats with their supervisors and collect their *Overtime* sheets from their supervisors.

11.57
LIGHT FACTORY song

12.00
Finish

Here is a listening game you can play at home:

Sit very quietly on the settee in your lounge. Close your eyes and keep them closed for one minute. Listen very carefully. Now open your eyes and write down or draw all the things you heard.

My name is

....

Draw a line to the people you like to talk and listen to.

My Pets

Dad

My Friends

Light Factory Supervisor

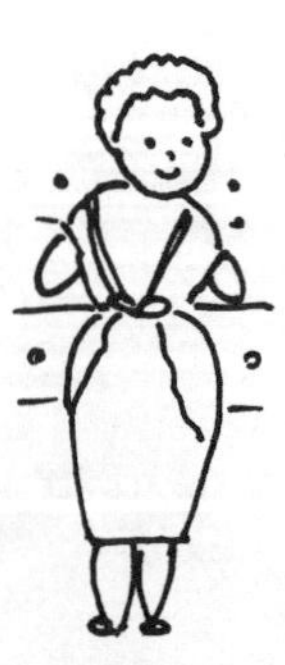

Mum

Jesus

Teacher

Mary, Martha and Lazarus were good friends with Jesus. The pictures below tell the story of what happened to these friends. Number the boxes in the correct order in which they happened.

Jesus listened and talked to Mary and Martha

Lazarus died

Mary and Martha asked Jesus to come

Everyone was amazed and very happy

Jesus came to see Mary and Martha

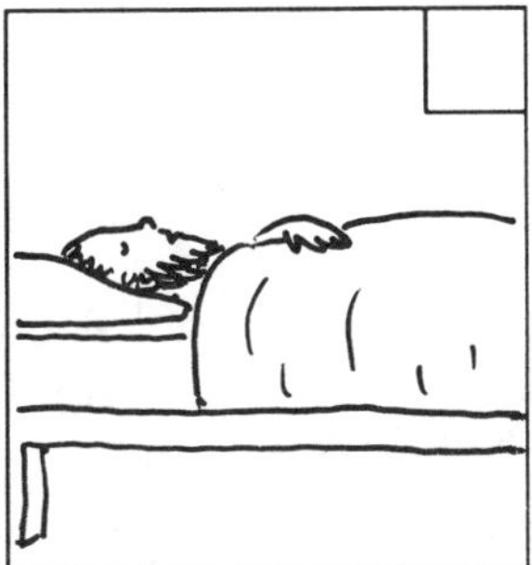
Lazarus was ill

Jesus brought Lazarus back to life

Jesus did not come straight away

CODE

a = ⟍	i = ◿	r = ▽
b = ⟋	j = △	s = ⧊
c = ┐	k = ⧄	t = ○
d = ┌	l = ⧅	u = ⦶
e = ⊓	m = ⊠	v = ⊖
f = ⊐	n = +	w = ⊗
g = □	o = ⍏	x = ⧖
h = ▷	p = ⍖	y = ⟠
	q = ∼	z = ⊕

Using the code, write the names of those who listen to you and who you listen to.

Those who listen to me are: ________

I listen to these people: ________

Find the eight words connected with friendship:

TALK	CARE
LISTEN	LIKE
CONVERSATION	SHARE
UNDERSTAND	TOUCH

(You can go up, down, backwards, forwards or diagonally.)

U	A	C	J	U	B	L	D	L	I	C
K	N	I	Y	X	I	F	T	O	D	O
L	N	D	E	K	X	T	A	L	K	N
W	M	E	E	H	C	T	M	I	C	V
Y	F	R	B	R	B	E	Z	N	T	E
E	R	A	C	U	S	I	H	K	O	R
E	V	H	L	I	S	T	E	N	W	S
G	U	S	O	A	G	F	A	R	H	A
T	O	U	C	H	G	Q	J	N	L	T
V	M	P	Q	U	M	A	D	S	D	I
Y	S	A	W	C	K	P	U	E	T	O
R	O	J	S	N	O	P	V	R	Z	N

All the words are about communicating. Most of the communicating we do with our friends involves listening and talking.
Write a list of all the things you listen to:

Who would you choose to talk about the following things to? (Circle the answer you most agree with in each case.)

A problem with homework	PARENT FRIEND GOD	TEACHER NO ONE
A new record you've just bought	PARENT FRIEND GOD	TEACHER NO ONE
Where to go on holiday	PARENT FRIEND GOD	TEACHER NO ONE
A rise in pocket money	PARENT FRIEND GOD	TEACHER NO ONE
An argument with a friend	PARENT FRIEND GOD	TEACHER NO ONE

WHY WOULD YOU TALK TO THOSE PARTICULAR PEOPLE?

JESUS LISTENED TO MARY, MARTHA AND LAZARUS BECAUSE HE CARED ABOUT THEM AND THOUGHT THEY WERE IMPORTANT

DO YOU THINK HE WANTS TO LISTEN TO YOU?

MARY AND MARTHA TALKED TO JESUS ABOUT WHAT THEY THOUGHT AND HOW THEY FELT AND ASKED FOR HIS HELP

DO YOU THINK YOU COULD TALK TO JESUS ABOUT ANYTHING?

An experience with the Light

Peter discovers how much Jesus loves him

Bible material
John 18:15–18; 25–27; John 21:1–19

Key character
Peter

Key verses
Psalm 145:8–9

Key aim
To present Jesus – the Light of the world – as the one who loves us unconditionally, as illustrated by Peter's experience.

TEAM BIBLE STUDY AND PRAYER

Pray
Thank God that he loves you and all the people involved in your LIGHT FACTORY.

Read
John 18:15–18; 25–27

Peter had given up a successful fishing business and travelled miles from home to be with Jesus. He had witnessed miracles, heard breath-taking teaching and had become one of Jesus' closest friends. He was one of the few to recognise who Jesus was. He had spent three years eating with, listening to and sharing with a man to whom he had pledged undying loyalty – yet at the time that Jesus needed him most, he failed. Peter denied all knowledge of the existence of his best friend. He allowed a fixed trial to take place without even speaking out against it. Finally, at the execution, he was nowhere to be seen.

Discuss
Close your eyes and try to imagine how Peter felt at the moment the cock crowed.

Read
John 21:1–19

A beautiful morning had dawned. Jesus was alive and all was right with the world – or was it? Not for Peter. There were too many reminders of the past. A familiar fishing trip. Jesus performing a miracle. The offer of breakfast on the beach and a chat with Jesus. The last time Peter smelled a charcoal fire was in a courtyard on the night he denied Jesus. He must had felt wretched. The final straw was to have a conversation with the friend he had let down so badly. Jesus didn't remind Peter of past failures – he just wanted to know that they were still friends. Peter almost choked before he had the courage to once more claim that he loved Jesus. He realised in the end that Jesus' love for him was totally unconditional. It had never changed – even in the middle of his greatest failure. This love removed failure and fear and restored confidence and certainty to a broken man.

Discuss
Do I need to be restored from failure and fear to confidence and certainty in the Light of the world?

Reflect
Jesus loves you. He couldn't love you any more or any less than he does at this very moment. He knows you the same today as he did when he died for you. Nothing will *ever* change his love. This is true for every child in your factory unit. They need to experience the same reflection of this unconditional love through you. This fourth visit to the LIGHT FACTORY should show them a love that can only be found in the Light of the world.

Pray
Read Psalm 145:8–9. Pray for each child in your factory unit and remember that the Lord is 'slow to become angry and full of constant love.' Ask him to help you to be like that today.

PROGRAMME AT A GLANCE

Time	Activity
10.15	Time-and-a-half
10.25	LIGHT FACTORY song
10.28	Welcome
10.30	T-break
10.37	Get-lit-go! explanation
10.39	Walk-on 1
10.40	Assembly line
11.00	Race through space
11.12	LIP service
11.16	Song(s)
11.20	Get-lit-go!
11.23	Walk-on 2
11.24	Work out
11.27	Laser challenge
11.35	Spotlight interview
11.39	Discussion
11.51	Comment
11.54	Newsflash/overtime
11.57	LIGHT FACTORY song
12.00	Finish

WHAT YOU WILL NEED

Registration
- Registration cards
- clocking-in cards
- clocking-in box
- date stamp

STAGE AREA
- LIGHT FACTORY cassette and/or music for songs
- Words to songs on overhead transparencies or large card
- Music cassette for *workout* (aerobics)
- Bible character: biblical costume for Peter, fishing net, water to pour on Peter, bread
- *Laser challenge: Laser challenge* bin, *Laser challenge* badges, bin liners, floor covering; three egg cups, three chairs, nine eggs, three protective goggles
- *Spotlight* interview questions and notes for comment
- Notices
- LIP service post box
- *Race through space*: quiz board and questions
- Drama serial: light bulb, duster, walkie-talkie radio

Units
- Programme at a glance
- Bible
- *Get-lit-go!* materials
- *Spotlight* discussion questions
- *Overtime* sheets
- Entry forms for *Laser challenge*
- Hats
- Felt pens or crayons and scissors for making hats.

Age groups
- Equipment and materials for activities
- games and crafts in age groups

Programme details

10.15
Time-and-a-half
Discuss *Overtime* sheets

10.25
LIGHT FACTORY song

10.28
Welcome
Welcome the workers and give a run-down of what's happening today.

10.30
T-break
Drama serial, episode 4

10.37
Get-lit-go! Explanation
Explain to the workers that, at the given signal, all workers must stand and each unit form a circle. Everyone then reaches across their circle with their right hand and joins right hands with one other person in the circle. They then reach across the circle and join left hands with a different person. Each unit must then 'untangle' themselves until they are once more in a circle. This must be done without letting go of their hands. (You might like to give them a practice of forming a circle and joining hands.)

10.39
Walk-on 1
Peter (in biblical dress) walks across the stage area whistling and carrying a fishing net. Presenters make comments such as 'Who was that?', 'What is he doing here?', etc.

10.40
Assembly line
Games, crafts, or activities in age groups.

11.00
Race through space
Presenters lead the workers in a quiz using the *Race through space* quiz board.

11.12
LIP service
Remind the workers this is their last day to post letters. Make any appropriate comments on letters received.

11.16
Song(s)
Choose from the cassette or from songs with which the workers are familiar.

11.20
Get-lit-go!
(previously explained)

11.23
Walk-on 2
Peter walks on with no net and now he is soaking wet and looks excited.

11.24
Workout
Factory keep-fit

11.27
Laser challenge
Presenters draw six names from the *Laser Challenge* bin. Place bin liners and protective goggles on three of the participants. Have them lie down, face up, on the floor. Place three chairs six inches beyond the tops of their heads with the backs of the chairs level with the point 6 inches beyond their heads. Place egg cups on their foreheads. The other three children are to kneel on the chairs with hands resting on the backs of the chairs. They are given three eggs each which they must break one at a time and attempt to land the egg in the egg cup below. You will need three leaders to replace any egg cups which fall off the workers' foreheads. Have water and towels ready for the children at the end of the challenge. Present the *Laser challenge* badges to the six participants.

11.35
Spotlight
Interview. Peter walks on eating bread and this time is stopped by the presenters and they proceed with the interview.

Main points to bring out. Ensure that the interview brings out Peter's feelings and reactions when he realised just how much Jesus loved him.

Bring out some of Peter's past: the fact he had followed Jesus but had denied him. After that, Jesus had been crucified but had risen from the dead and then met up with Peter again.

Begin the story of Peter and Jesus' conversation on the beach. This conversation was surprising because Peter had let Jesus down so badly. The reason that Jesus and Peter could restore their relationship was because of Jesus' death and resurrection bringing forgiveness. Keep reinforcing the depth of Jesus' love for Peter.

Interview questions. Use these questions as a basis to give Peter the opportunity to develop the main point:

- How did you get wet?
- Are you a friend of Jesus?
- Have you ever let him down?
- Was he angry with you?
- What happened to Jesus?
- If he died, how come he was on the beach?
- What have you been talking about?
- Why did he keep asking if you loved him?
- How does this make you feel?

Discussion in units. (11.39) Workers are given the opportunity to enter their names for the *Laser challenge*.

Discussion questions.

5–7s

- What makes you feel excited?
- Why was Peter so excited to see Jesus?
- What had Peter done that made Jesus sad?
- What did Jesus say to Peter?
- Do you think that they were friends again?

7–11s

- Has a friend ever let you down?
- How did you feel?
- Did you find it hard to forgive him or her?
- Do you think Jesus found it hard to forgive Peter?

11–14s

- Has a friend ever let you down?
- How did you feel?
- Was the relationship ever put right?
- Would you have liked (a) Jesus (b) Peter as a friend?
- Why?

Spotlight comment (11.51). Presenter draws the attention of the units to the front and gives closing comments.

The presenter should take this opportunity to summarise today's learning and develop the idea that Jesus loved Peter unconditionally. He/she should explain the situation something like the following:

Peter had always been one of Jesus' closest friends. He had always defended him and been loyal. I expect that one of the worst things he thought anyone could do was to let a friend down – yet he did it. He must have hated himself. So he must have been absolutely amazed to discover that Jesus still cared about him and still wanted to be his friend. Jesus just wanted to know if Peter loved him – after all, Jesus still loved Peter.

Jesus might be asking that question of us and we need to think about it. It doesn't matter if we think we've let Jesus down, he still loves us and wants to be our friend.

Use this opportunity to invite the children to talk over anything they are confused by, concerned about or challenged by with their supervisor.

11.54
Newsflash/overtime
Notices. Remind the workers to leave their hats and collect their *Overtime* sheets from their supervisors.

11.57
LIGHT FACTORY song

12.00
Finish

Jesus cooked fish and bread for breakfast.

Peter and the other fishermen had breakfast with Jesus.

Draw the fish and bread on their plates.

Peter loved Jesus and they were friends.

Do you know anyone who loves Jesus?

Write their names in this box.

My name is ....

T R A P B U F H P D U T N E C
S S E T F M I J R S N I F I Q
A C P E T E R P K Q A E J B R
F E R D K Z E L T S B L T R N
K Q H C G I D A R F G A K E R
A G A P F O C N O L O V E N O
E Y E O A I E N Q B I K L G M
R X J E S U S G H E J M U T L
B F D B W C N H I A V O E K B
E O R I A D G I A C J B L A R
T G M L O A D C K H E I K V E
A M U G F E C D R M K H O T A
P E L E B C A H U I F R J J D

Can you find these words in the box?

PETER
JESUS
FISH
BREAD
BEACH
FIRE
LOVE
NET
BOAT
BREAKFAST

Light Fax

In the Light Factory we have been learning about people who have loved Jesus and were his friends. Here are the names of two of them. Can you write the names of others we learned about?

JOHN

MARY

Do you know anyone who loves Jesus and is a friend of his? Write their names here.

OVERTIME 4

11-14s

Draw a cartoon which describes what love is.
For example:

Love is...
Being together

We love people in lots of different ways, not just romantically. Jesus showed how much he loved Peter by forgiving him for letting him down at the time when Jesus needed him most.

THERE IS NOTHING WE CAN EVER DO THAT WILL STOP JESUS LOVING US

HOW DO YOU THINK JESUS FELT WHEN PETER DENIED HIM?

HOW DO YOU THINK PETER FELT WHEN JESUS FORGAVE HIM

The following people have all hurt someone close to them. Write down how you think the hurt person should react if he or she really loved the person who has hurt them.

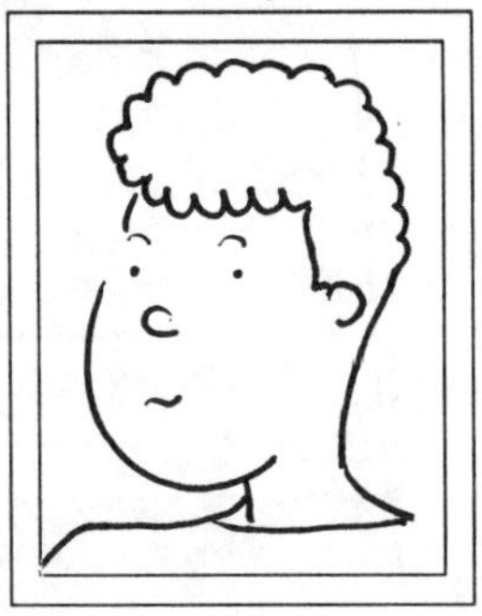

Steve has been going out with Tracey, his best friend's girlfriend, behind his back. Terry, his best friend, has just found out.

Jane has told everyone at school that her friend Alison's parents have just got divorced.

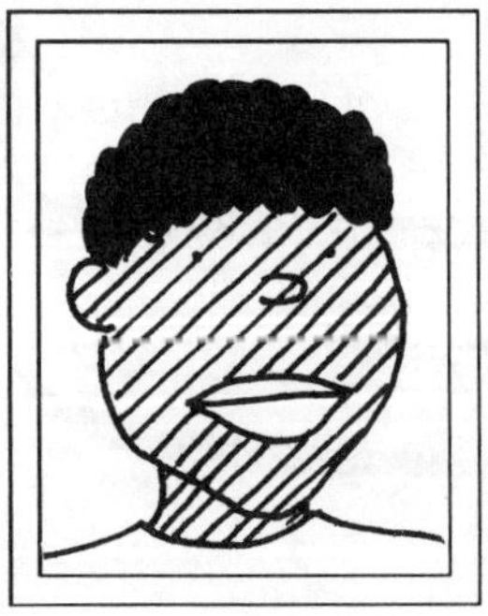

Lee has just been refused a paper round because he's black. The newsagent is the dad of Lee's best friend.

What should Terry do?

What should Alison do?

What should Lee do?

Would you have found it hard to forgive in any of these situations?

NO ☐ YES ☐ If YES, which one(s) 1 ☐ 2 ☐ 3 ☐

Belonging to the Light

Jesus' light still shines today

Bible material
John 1:1–5; John 12:44–46

Key character
A Supervisor

Key verse
Psalm 27

Key aim
To present Jesus – the Light of the world – as the person to whom the key characters belong and to whom we can also belong.

TEAM BIBLE STUDY AND PRAYER

Pray
Thank God for Jesus – the Light of the world.

Read
John 1:1–5

Jesus – the Light of the world – existed before the world even began. He was involved in its creation, lived in our time and on our planet and will shine as the Light of the world long after the earth ceases to exist. Jesus – the Light of the world – shattered the spiritual darkness throughout the whole of history and will continue to do so after the end of time. The picture of Jesus as the Light of the world has incredible implications that most of us could never explain or even understand. Jesus knew that – so instead of just telling us he was the Light of the world he became it. He demonstrated who the Light of the world was by the things he did. Jesus didn't just say things – he showed what they meant by the way he lived.

Discuss
What sort of things did Jesus do that showed he was the Light of the world?

Read
John 12:44–46

Jesus brought light to dark places as we have seen in our key characters this week. Throughout the ages Christians have suffered persecution and death in order to reflect that Light. John the Baptist, the Samaritan woman, Mary, Martha, Lazarus and Peter have all reflected something of the Light of the world to us. And now it's our turn.

How can I reflect the Light of the world to my factory unit and others?

Reflect
The light shines on and will never be put out. We belong to the Light of the world, just as our key characters did. When we belong to him, we can reflect Jesus to the rest of the world. This fifth visit to the LIGHT FACTORY gives an opporunity for the children to find out what it means to belong to the Light of the world.

Pray
Ask God to help you to make it clear what it means to belong to the Light of the world. Ask him to help you to be light in your unit. Read Psalm 27 together as a statement of your confidence in Jesus, the Light of the world, today.

PROGRAMME AT A GLANCE

Time	Activity
10.15	Time-and-a-half
10.25	LIGHT FACTORY song
10.28	Welcome
10.31	Assembly line
10.51	Get-lit-go! explanation
10.54	T-break 1
11.00	Walk-on 1
11.01	Workout
11.04	Laser challenge
11.12	Walk-on 2
11.13	Get-lit-go!
11.16	T-break 2
11.22	LIP service
11.26	Song(s)
11.31	Spotlight interview
11.35	Discussion
11.47	Comment and candle-lighting
11.55	Newsflash
11.57	LIGHT FACTORY song
12.00	Finish

WHAT YOU WILL NEED

Registration
- Registration cards
- clocking-in cards
- clocking-in box
- date stamp

Stage area
- LIGHT FACTORY cassette and/or music for songs
- Words to songs on overhead transparencies or large card
- Music cassette for *workout* (aerobics)
- Walk-on character: macintosh, sunglasses, hat
- *Laser challenge: Laser challenge* bin, *Laser challenge* badges, bin liners, floor covering; three pots of bubbles with blowers, three full water pistols
- *Spotlight* interview questions and notes for comment
- Notices
- LIP service post box
- Drama serial: part 5: pencil and paper; part 6: keys, flashing light

Units
- Programme at a glance
- Bible
- *Get-lit-go!* Three dried peas and a drinking straw for each worker in every unit
- *Spotlight* discussion questions
- Hats
- Felt pens or crayons and scissors for making hats

Age groups
- Equipment and materials for activities
- games and crafts in age groups

Programme details

10.15
Time-and-a-half
Discuss *Overtime* sheets.

10.25
LIGHT FACTORY song

10.28
Welcome
Welcome the workers and give a run-down of what's happening today.

10.31
Assembly line
Games, crafts, or activities in age groups.

10.51
Get-lit-go! Explanation
Once *Assembly line* is finished and the workers are back in their units, the presenters explain that at the given signal all workers, in their units, must get into a straight line. Supervisors will then give each of them a drinking straw. One at a time they must go to the supervisor who is standing ten feet from the queue and collect a pea which the supervisor is holding. They are to do this by sucking through the drinking straw so the pea stays at the end of the straw. They must walk around the supervisor once without losing the pea and drop it back in the supervisor's hand. Each unit gives a loud cheer once everyone in the unit has completed the task. Supervisors collect up all the drinking straws.

10.54
T-break 1
Drama serial, episode 5

11.00
Walk-on 1
A supervisor, 'in disguise', (ie sunglasses, mac, hat etc.) walks across the stage.

11.01
Workout
Factory keep-fit

11.04
Laser challenge
Presenters draw the names of six children out of the Challenge bin. Three are given a bottle of bubbles each and the other three water pistols. The three with the bubbles are to stand at the front of the stage area, five feet apart and side-on to the units. The three with the water pistols are to stand ten feet behind them towards the back of the stage area. At a given signal the three at the front are to start blowing bubbles in the air and the three at the back try to shoot as many bubbles as possible. They are to work as partners with the one at the back shooting the bubbles of the one directly in front of him/her. You will need three supervisors to act as counters of 'bubble hits'. They should be given one minute for this challenge. (Some workers at the front may get slightly wet.) Present the *Laser challenge* badges to the six participants.

11.12
Walk-on 2
As before.

11.13
Get-lit-go!
As previously explained.

11.16
T-break 2
Drama serial, episode 6

11.22
LIP service
Make any appropriate comments on any letters received.

11.26
Song(s)
Choose from the cassette or from songs with which the workers are familiar.

11.31
Spotlight
Interview. Supervisor walks on again and this time is stopped by the presenters who should gradually reveal who the mystery guest is by questioning him/her. When the workers realise who it is the disguise should be removed. (Many of the younger children will probably expect it to be a Bible character.)

Main points to bring out. Ensure that the interview brings out that people today can belong to Jesus, the Light of the world, just as the biblical characters did.

The presenter should ask questions that eventually enable the children to guess the identity of the mystery guest. The key character should help in summing up the week's activities and learning, for instance, how she first learned that Jesus was the

Light of the world. She could perhaps share an incident that illustrates how well Jesus knows her; how she is able to talk to him about anything; how she experiences his love; how Jesus speaks to her. She should take the opportunity to re-emphasise that Jesus is alive today and can be a friend to us.

Interview questions.

- How old are you?
- What colour are your eyes?
- Are you a man or a woman?
- What is your job in the LIGHT FACTORY?
- OR any other questions that reveal something unique, about the person, which will help the children recognise him/her.
- Everyone else we have met this week was in the Bible, so why are *you* here?
- Do you believe that Jesus is the Light of the world?
- How do you know?
- Can anybody belong to Jesus?

Discussion in units (11.35). Today's discussion questions are the same for everyone:

- What sort of a person is Jesus?
- What have you learned about him this week?
- Who do you know who belongs to Jesus?
- How can people belong to Jesus, the Light of the world?

Be prepared for each age group to respond at their own level. All their responses to God are valid, however simple or seemingly unconnected to some of the things *we* want them to learn.

Spotlight comment and candle-lighting (11.47). Presenter draws the attention of the units to the front and gives closing comments. This 'comment' takes the form of the presenter involving the whole factory in order to sum up what has been learned this week.

For safety purposes ensure all children have removed their hats and the hats have been set to one side. Have fire extinguishers or buckets of water nearby. Ensure all candles have holders to avoid burns from hot wax.

One presenter should hold a large, lighted candle. He/she should explain that we have learnt lots this week about Jesus being the Light of the world. He was God's son, so that when people met him, they found out what God was like. All kinds of people belonged to Jesus, John the Baptist; the Samaritan woman; Mary, Martha and Lazarus and Peter. (As each one is mentioned, they should come on stage and light a small candle from the large one.)

It wasn't only the people who met Jesus when he was on earth who belonged to the Light of the world, but people right through history – even people today. (All the supervisors should light candles from the large one.) The people in the Bible spread Jesus' light and helped others to discover how they could belong to the Light and spread it too; that is why it is still spreading today.

If you belong to Jesus, you, too, can help spread his light. (The supervisors should give a candle to each factory worker in their unit who light them from the supervisor's candle.) Jesus, the Light of the world, is the one who knows all about us, listens, understands and talks to us and always loves us.

This may be an appropriate point to pray (asking the children to keep their eyes open for safety), and/or invite the children to talk to their supervisor if they want to know more about belonging to the Light, or anything else that is on their mind.

11.55
Newsflash
Notices of any family service, Sunday school, etc. Remind the children to take their hats, etc home with them.

11.57
LIGHT FACTORY song

12.00
Finish

Drama serial
THE LIGHTHOUSE

SUMMARY

Scene
A lighthouse in outer space. The only scenery needed is a window suspended at one side of the stage (a hoop covered in silver foil with curtains that can be drawn), a table and a chair. Some means of flashing the stage lights will be useful for episode 6.

Characters
Glad. The factory cleaner who is a cheery and endearing character. She is the link between the lighthouse and the Light Factory.

Costume. Dress and apron, a few curlers in her hair, feather duster or dust cloth.

Albert. The lighthouse keeper. A 'real character'; old and set in his ways. He is kindly in intent but somewhat gruff in manner. (There's no doubt about who's running the show!) He has a great sense of importance and doesn't do much work himself but orders his helpers around with great gusto. Years of living away from society have narrowed his mind and made him a little eccentric.

Costume. Sou'wester or captain's hat, chunky-knit jumper, baggy trousers, wellies.

Slap and Tickle. Albert's helpers. As the story unfolds we discover Slap is bad and Tickle is good. They are comic characters with an endless supply of tricks to play on one another. They have boundless energy and as well as the fun they have they work hard to keep the lighthouse going. Slap is the Communicatons Officer and Tickle tends the light.

Costumes. Fishermen's smocks or tee-shirts of two different colours, and trousers. (Do not use black and white to signify bad and good.)

Rep. The representative from the Light Council. Enigmatic and young, a contrast to Albert. Fun and trendy but not in a superficial or self-conscious way.

Costume. Bright, colourful clothing.

Episodes
Episode 1. The scene is set and the characters introduced with their various jobs. Some fun and games are had with Slap and Tickle. When the audience is familiar with the setting it is revealed that the lighthouse is in fact out in space guarding the entrance to the black hole. So far it has succeeded and no spaceship has strayed into it. The episode ends with Albert's attention being caught by something unusual happening outside. What could it be?

Episode 2. There is a great deal of activity around the black hole. They've never seen anything like it before. What is worse is that many spaceships seem to be disappearing into it. Tickle checks the light to make sure that it is operating effectively, which it is. Albert notices that there seem to be lights rather like their own coming out of the black hole. In fact the lights are so confusing that spaceships can no longer tell where the black hole is and so are drawn into it. The phoney lights are rendering Albert's lighthouse totally ineffective. Albert finds this disturbing as he thought that his light was a special one with a secret frequency that could not be reproduced. Slap offers to tune in on his walkie-talkie radio and find out what's happening. We discover that Slap is in communication with Invader Forces and is passing on the secret frequency to them. What will happen? Will Albert discover the spy in the camp?

Episode 3. Tickle is trying to cheer Albert up but only succeeds in upsetting him more by arguing with Slap. While Tickle is looking out of the window he notices strange flashing lights coming from the sky. He senses that they are trying to communicate and it may be an offer of help. Albert is immediately suspicious and thinks it is a trick of the Invader Forces or even another black hole forming. He pulls the curtains and forbids anyone to look again, which obviously pleases Slap. Things appear to be going from bad to worse, what can they do?

Episode 4. Rep, a representative from the Light Council, calls on the lighthouse. Being aware of the problem, he offers help. Rep explains that if the lighthouse were plugged into their circuit it would produce a super-duper-dark-shattering light. Albert, Slap and Tickle could continue to live and work in the lighthouse but would have to hand over the keys to the Light Council. Albert is none too happy about handing over control of his beloved lighthouse and stubbornly refuses to agree. Slap convinces Albert that Rep is trying to steal the lighthouse and that they must get rid of him. Albert agrees and leaves it to Slap to send their unwelcome guest off the premises. Slap sends him in the direction of the black hole.

Episode 5. Tickle can't help thinking about what Rep said and he goes to the window to have another look at the strange flashing lights. He realises the lights are flashing in morse code and enlists Albert's help to decipher the message. The decoded message is 'sing the lighthouse song', but they don't know what this means without Rep's help. At this point, Slap reveals he sent Rep in the direction of the black hole and tampered with the light so that they, too, are being drawn into the black hole. Will they escape?

Episode 6. The light in the lighthouse is fading and there doesn't seem to be anything they can do to stop it. Their only hope is in Rep. With the help of the factory workers, Tickle and Albert learn the song which brings Rep back to the lighthouse. He has survived the black hole because he has the super-duper-darkness-shattering light. Albert hands over the keys to the lighthouse, they plug into the new circuit and the lighthouse is saved.

Lighthouse Song

(To go with Light Factory Drama Serial)

Light-house, Light-house shin - ing bright Plugged in, switched on, do - ing all right

Light-house, Light-house shin - ing bright With a su - per - du - per - dark-shat-t'ring light.

Lighthouse, Lighthouse shining bright
Plugged in, switched on, doing all right
Lighthouse, Lighthouse shining bright
With a super-duper-dark-shattering light.

THE LIGHTHOUSE

(Daily episodes)

(*Enter Glad, the cleaner.*)

Glad Hello! Tea break in the factory is it? (*Workers encouraged by supervisors to respond 'Yes'*) That's good! I'm Glad. I mean . . . well, that's my name . . . Glad. I'm the factory cleaner. I bet you didn't know the Light Factory had a cleaner. Well it does and I'm it. But enough of that because now it's time to take you on a journey. Not just any old journey, though. We're going to a lighthouse. But before we go there's something we need to learn. Every time you hear the words 'the black hole' you have to shout 'NOT THE BLACK HOLE!' Let's have a practice . . . 'The black hole' (*workers respond*). Right, this time a little louder . . . 'The black hole' (*workers respond*). That was great! You might hear those words at any time, so better be on your toes! Right, now we're off to the lighthouse. There are three people who live in the lighthouse. The lighthouse keeper is Albert. Then there's Slap and Tickle – what a pair! Anyway, off we go.
(*Exit Glad.*)

(*Enter Albert.*)

Albert This place could do with a clean. Where are those two young rascals? Slap! Tickle! Come here.

(*Enter Slap and Tickle larking about.*)

Albert This place is a mess. I want one of you to sweep up and one of you to dust and I'd like it done before I get back.

Slap Why, where are you going Albert?

Albert I'm going for forty winks . . . I mean I'm off to think . . . Oh! It's none of your business. Just get busy!
(*Exit Albert.*)

Tickle Right, Slap, you sweep and I'll dust.

Slap All right.
(*Slap picks up broom and starts to dust things with it. Tickle wipes floor with duster.*)

Tickle No, that's not right. Gimme that broom!
(*Reverse happens.*)

Tickle Oh, you! I suppose you think that's funny!
(Slap giggles slyly; both do the proper jobs.)

Tickle You know, I'm glad I came to work here. I mean, it's not everybody who gets to look after the light in a lighthouse in outer space.

Slap Pooh! Looking after a light's nothing special. Being Communications Officer is much more fun and far more important.

Tickle Trust you to give it a fancy name! All you do is talk to spaceships on a walkie-talkie radio.

Slap Yeah, but I'm the one who warns them about the black hole (*'Not the black hole!'*)

Tickle But if it wasn't for my light they wouldn't be able to see which way to go.

Slap But I could tell them . . .

Albert (*offstage*) Slap, Tickle, have you finished in there?

Slap Quick, look busy! (To Albert) Just about.
(Albert enters. Slap and Tickle lean on broom and table)

Albert Oh, that looks better. Much more like home. I always say that 'once a place has been tidied, it's a nicer place to live in'. (Slap and Tickle mouth words in inverted commas)

Slap Pity you don't do any tidying yourself then.
(Tickle nudges Slap in ribs.)

Albert What was that?

Slap (*Hasty grin.*) Oh, er, it's a pity Tickle didn't dust the shelf then.

Albert Oh, he didn't?

Tickle (*withering look at Slap*) I'll do it now.
(Albert inspects room. Looks out of window.)

Albert Ah, this is the life. I can't think of a better way to live than out here in the middle of the universe guarding the entrance to the black hole. (*'Not the black hole!'*) In fact I enjoy it so much, I don't think I ever want to go home. I'd like to stay out here for ever, surrounded by nothing but space, helping ships in distress, and keeping them from straying into the black hole. (*'Not the black hole!'*)
(As Albert says this, Slap is creeping up on Tickle, who is still dusting, to play some nasty trick. Just as he is about to do it . . .)

Albert (*Shouts*) Hey! What's happening? Come here and look, you two!
(Slap and Tickle go to the window. All freeze.)

(Enter Glad.)

Glad Well, what do you think Albert has seen? It certainly made Slap and Tickle jump! But we'll just have to wait until tomorrow to find out. (*Exit Albert, Slap, Tickle.*)

Before I go there's a special song I'd like to teach you. It's a special lighthouse song and it goes like this. (*Sing Lighthouse song and teach it to the workers.*) Do you think you can remember that until tomorrow? ('Yes!') Right. See you then.
(Exit Glad.)

(Enter Glad.)

Glad Hello, Factory workers! Glad the cleaner here. In a minute we're going to the lighthouse, but first let's see if you remember the special lighthouse song I taught you. (*Sing lighthouse song.*)

Great! Well, can you remember how we left Albert, Slap and Tickle? (*They enter and resume last positions.*) They were all looking out of the window at something that Albert had spotted near the black hole. (*'Not the . . .!'*) Anyway, let's find out what he's seen.
(Exit Glad.)
(Unfreeze.)

Tickle What have you seen, Albert?

Slap Is it invading aliens? Have you got a laser beam we can blast them with?

Albert Don't be silly. Aliens don't come within a light year of *my* lighthouse. But it's very odd. Can you see all those spaceships around the black hole? (*'Not the . . .!'*) I've never seen so many!

Tickle OOH, aah (*etc.*)
(Slap looks secretly pleased with himself..)

Tickle Ooh, Albert, that spaceship's disappeared! I think it's been swallowed up by the black hole! (*'Not the. . .!'*)

Albert Tickle, I think you're right! What's gone wrong with the lighthouse? We're supposed to stop spaceships doing that!

Tickle Shall I check the light, Albert? Maybe it's broken down.

Albert I doubt that *my* light would break down but, yes, go and check all the same.
(Exit Tickle.)

Slap Strange, isn't it?

Albert What is?

Slap Spaceships going into the black hole. (*'Not the . . .!'*)

Albert Yes, it is. I'd like to know what's causing it.

Slap Would you now? Er, I mean, yeah, so would I!
(Enter Tickle.)

Tickle No, the light's working great! Shining away just like it always has. Are the spaceships being sucked in?

Albert Yes . . . Hey! I've just noticed something. Come and look, Tickle! Can you see that light coming *out* of the black hole? (*'Not the . . .!'*)

Tickle Oooh, yeah! Isn't it weird?

Albert Slap, does it look familiar to you?

Slap Me? Er, no, no, not familiar at all.

Tickle Hey! It looks just like *our* light – from this lighthouse!

Albert That's what I thought. Somehow, someone has made the same light as us, and now all the spaceships are getting confused, and going the wrong way!

Tickle But that's impossible. I thought our light was a special one with a secret frequency that nobody can copy! Right, Slap?

Slap What? Oh yes, right. Why don't you go and check the light again? Perhaps someone's been meddling with it!

Tickle Ooh, they'd better not! Just wait till I catch them!

Slap I'll see if I can find out what's going on. I'll radio out a message.

Albert I'll come with you Tickle.
(*Exit Albert and Tickle.*)

(*Slap gets out radio.*)

Slap Slap to Invader Forces. Are you there? . . . Yeah, it's working! All the spaceships are being sucked into the black hole. ('*Not the* . . .!') I don't think you've got the light frequency quite right. Just turn it up ten megawatts, that should do it. Hey, I'd better go, I think they're coming back.
(*Puts radio up and freezes.*)
(*Enter Glad.*)

Glad Well, Well! What a little toad Slap's turning out to be! Do you think Albert will ever find out? I hope so! But we'll have to wait until tomorrow to see! And, remember, keep practicing that song I taught you. Who knows, it might come in handy!
(*Exit Glad and Slap.*)

(*Enter Glad.*)

Glad Can you remember what happened yesterday? We'd just found out that Slap is a spy for Invader Forces. He's helping them confuse all the spaceships so they're being sucked into the black hole. ('*Not the* . . .!') And Albert is so upset. How about singing the lighthouse song? Maybe that'll get Albert into a better mood. (*Sing lighthouse song.*)
(*Exit Glad.*)

(*Enter Slap and Tickle and Albert. Tickle taps Albert on shoulder, gets behind him, moves same way he moves. Albert finds him but it doesn't cheer him up..*)

Tickle Oh, come on Albert! Cheer up! It's not the end of the world!

Albert It may as well be. My lighthouse isn't working properly and the spaceships are being sent into the black hole. ('*Not the* . . .!') What is there to be cheerful about?

Slap He's right. You'd be more help polishing your precious light bulb.

Tickle Oh, shut up, you! You're not being much help yourself. You didn't find an answer to our problems when you radioed out yesterday.

Slap Yes, but at least I . . .

Albert Oh give it a rest, the pair of you! I can't stand all this bickering. I'm going upstairs.
(*Exit Albert.*)

Slap Now see what you've done. You've upset him now.

Tickle Oh, you . . .
(*Turns to window.*)

Slap Anyway, I don't see what all the fuss is about. I mean, it's only a bit of light when all's said and done, and who's going to worry about a little bit of light?

Tickle Shut up a minute, Slap, and come and look at this.

Slap Look at what? You mean the black hole? ('*Not the* . . .!')

Tickle No, not the black hole ('*Not the* . . .!') Look, there are some strange flashing lights over there. I don't understand. What do you think they are?
(*Slap looks horrified – tries to cover up.*)

Slap Oh, I don't think it's anything special. Probably just another spaceship.

Tickle No, it's not. It's stayed in the same place all the time. Ooh, I can't explain it; those lights make me tingle all over like they want to help or they are trying to get some message through to us – but I can't understand what they're saying!

Slap What a load of rubbish! They're not saying anything. They're just a load of fairy lights.

Tickle Well, I don't think they are. I'm going to fetch Albert and see what he thinks.
(*Exit Tickle.*)

Slap Drat! This could spoil my plans. If those lights are what I think they are, I'm in trouble.

(*Enter Tickle and Albert.*)

Tickle Come on, Albert. You can see them out of the window – look! Can you see?

Albert Oh, yes, I can see them all right. But it might be another trick from the Invader Forces.

Tickle Oh, no, Albert. Can't you feel they want to help us?

Albert Load of nonsense. How could flashing lights help us? No, more likely it means trouble for us. Probably the beginning of another black hole. ('*Not the . . .!*') Anyway, I don't want anybody else looking out of the window.

Slap Good idea, Albert.

Albert We've seen quite enough nasty things from there.

Slap Oh, definitely.
(*Albert pulls curtains. Freezes.*)

(*Enter Glad.*)

Glad So, things seem to be going from bad to worse for the poor old lighthouse. I thought they were going to get some help for a minute, but Albert and Slap soon put a stop to that. He's a nasty piece of work, that Slap. Anyway, you'll have to wait until tomorrow to find out if any help does come. See you then!
(*Exit all.*)

(*Enter Tickle, Slap and Albert. Tickle looks miserable. Slap looks smug. Albert looks worried. Tickle polishes a light bulb. Slap fiddles with radio. Albert sits in chair with chin on hands. All freeze.*)

(*Enter Glad.*)

Glad Well, here we are again. I don't think anything's improved since yesterday. Spaceships are still disappearing into the black hole ('*Not the . . .!*') and Albert, Slap and Tickle still haven't found a way to stop them. Have you remembered the song? (*Sing the song together.*) That's good!
Now, let's see what they're up to.
(*Exit Glad.*)

(*Tickle paces back and forth, Slap sits on the table, Albert stays in chair.*)

Tickle Oh this is boring. I wish you'd let us look out of the window, Albert.

Slap Oh shut up about the window. There's nothing to see anyway but the black hole. ('*Not the . . .!*')

Tickle But even that's better than nothing. Aren't you bored too, Albert?

Albert Bored? No. Too much on my mind.
(*Knock at the door.*)

Albert I wonder who that is? I hope it's not the lighthouse inspector – he's not due for another six months yet. Oh, answer the door, will you Tickle? I can't be bothered to get up.
(*Exit Tickle.*)

Albert Well, Slap, we're in a right mess. What are we going to do?
(*Enter Tickle and Rep – Rep is whistling or humming the lighthouse song.*)

Tickle Hey, Albert, look who's here! He says his name is Rep.

Albert Oh; a Rep, is he? What's he want?

Rep I understand you've had a few problems lately. Isn't your lighthouse supposed to be guarding the black hole? ('*Not the . . .!*')

Albert Well, yes . . .

Rep And stopping spaceships from vanishing into it?

Albert Well, yes. But . . .

Rep And it's not doing a very good job lately, right? That's why I've come. I can offer you a new electric circuit which will give you a new super-duper-dark-shattering light.

Slap A . . . a dark-shattering light?

Rep That's right. No more worries about the black hole! ('*Not the . . .!*')

Albert Oh yes? And how much does this super-duper-dark-shattering light cost?

Rep Nothing. It's free.

Slap/Tickle/Albert Free?!

Rep Free. But – you would have to give us the keys to your lighthouse. We'd still let you live and work here, of course. And the light would never, ever go wrong.

Albert But in order to get this light, I'd have to give the keys of *my* lighthouse to the Light Council?

Rep A small price to pay.

Albert But it's *my* lighthouse. It's *always* been my lighthouse!

Slap (*Stands.*) That's right, you can't expect Albert to give his keys up. It's his lighthouse.

Tickle Oh, but Albert. Can't you see? If we got this light everything would be all right. We wouldn't need to worry about the black hole. ('*Not the . . .!*') And we could live here for ever!

Slap Don't listen, Albert. They're just trying to steal your lighthouse.

Albert Yes, you are. You're trying to steal my lighthouse, Mr Rep, whoever you are. I'm having none of it. Get away with you and take your light with you. Slap – show him out.

Slap With pleasure.

(*Slap leads the Rep, whistling or humming lighthouse song, to opposite side of stage. Says, 'Keep going straight on', and pushes him offstage. Chuckles wickedly.*)

Slap (*To children – Tickle and Albert don't hear.*): Well, that's got rid of him! I've sent him into the black hole! ('*Not the . . .!*')

(*Freeze.*)

(*Enter Glad.*)

Glad Oh dear! Things aren't going at all well for Tickle and Albert! Slap's just getting his own way all the time and making things worse. I thought the Rep had the answer then, but Albert was so stubborn. Oh, well, we'll have to wait until tomorrow to see what happens. (*Exit Albert, Slap, Tickle.*)

Now, before I go I think we'd better have a practice of our song. (*Sing lighthouse song.*)

See you tomorrow!

(*Exit Glad.*)

DAY 5

(episode 1)

(*Enter Glad.*)

Glad Well, here we are again! Can you remember what happened yesterday? Albert met the Rep, who offered them a super-duper-dark-shattering light but Albert told Slap to send the Rep away, and he promptly sent him into the black hole. ('*Not the . . .!*') Now who's going to help save the lighthouse?

Before we start, let's have a practise of our Lighthouse song.

(*Exit Sing lighthouse song.*) Right, off we go!

(*Exit Glad.*)

(*Enter Slap and Tickle.*)

Tickle Oh, it's no good, Slap! I just can't help thinking about what the Rep said. If only Albert hadn't sent him away!

Slap Well, he did. And good riddance! All that rubbish about a super-duper light!

Tickle How do you know it was rubbish? If Albert had just agreed to give up the keys to the lighthouse we might not be in this mess.

Slap No, we might be in a worse one.

Tickle Oh, be quiet, you misery! I wish Albert would let us look out of the window. I'd love to see those flashing lights again. They were so reassuring, somehow.

Slap What a load of rubbish you speak, Tickle!

Tickle I don't care what Albert says, I'm having another look at the lights.

Slap If you do, I'll tell Albert.

Tickle Go and tell him then! But I'm having another look.

(*Tickle goes to window. Exit Slap.*)

Tickle Oooh, that's better! It's great to see them flashing away. Three short flashes, one long, one short, hey! Maybe it's a signal! That code stuff – morse code! Yes, that must be what it is. Albert'll know!

(*Enter Albert and Slap.*)

Albert Tickle, I told you not to . . .

Tickle Albert, do you know morse code?

Albert Well, a little bit. I was a Cub Scout, you know. Why?

Tickle Well, you know the special flashing lights. . . .?

Albert Yes, yes . . . Ah! But I told you before . . .

Tickle But, Albert, wait! This is really important. I'm sure it's something to do with the lighthouse.

Albert The lighthouse? Ah, well, that's different. Let's have a look then.

Slap Albert, it might be dangerous!

Albert Dangerous? What could be dangerous about a few flashing lights and a bit of morse code? Come on, Tickle. Now let's see. Three short flashes, that means '*S*'. Next letter is '*I*', '*N*', '*G*'. Tickle, write this down. (*Continues to decode:.*) '*THE LIGHT-HOUSE SONG*' 'Sing the lighthouse song', what lighthouse song? I don't know any lighthouse song. Oh, well, that was a waste of time!

Tickle Wait a minute! I think it has something to do with that Rep. I'm sure he could have helped us!

Albert Maybe you're right, Tickle. Maybe he will come back.

Slap Oh, no he won't, not from where I sent him.

Tickle What do you mean?

Slap He's gone for good. I sent him into the black hole ('*Not the . . .!*') and that's where we're going too!

Albert What do you mean, that's where we're going too?

Slap I've fiddled about with the supply light and started the lighthouse moving. Now *nothing* can stop us getting sucked in (*wicked laugh*). (*Freeze.*)

(*Enter Glad.*)

Glad What about that, then? I knew that Slap was up to no good. And now he's got the lighthouse moving towards the black hole. ('*Not the . . .!*') Do you think they can ever escape? We'll find out later. (*Exit all.*)

(episode 2)

(*Enter Albert, Slap and Tickle. Resume last positions.*)
(*Enter Glad.*)

Glad Well, when we left the lighthouse it was teetering on the edge of the black hole. ('*Not the . . .!*') How will they ever get out of this one? Let's see what they're up to. And . . . oh . . . you do remember the song, don't you? Good!
(*Exit Glad.*)

Albert Do you mean that you are in charge of the black hole ('*Not the . . .!*') and that it's *your* fault all the spaceships are being sucked in?

Slap No, I'm not in charge, but I do know who is. And it *is* my fault all the spaceships are being sucked in. And I'm *glad*. This is a silly lighthouse anyway.

Tickle Oh, if only the Rep were here! We could do with some of that super-duper-dark-shattering light just now. And if only those flashing lights had helped. (*To audience.*) But, I just can't understand what that morse code message means, 'Sing the lighthouse song'. What on earth does 'Sing the lighthouse song' mean?

Supervisors and workers We know!

Tickle Really? Do you know the song? Will you help me sing it? Go on then! (*Sing song.*)

Tickle Hey, that's the song the Rep was whistling (humming). Hey, Albert and Slap! Listen to this! Come on, sing it again.
(*Sing song again. Pause.*)

Tickle That *is* the song the Rep was whistling (humming)! I'm sure, if we all sing it, help will come.

Slap I'm not singing any silly song! (*Sulks.*)

Albert Well, I'll certainly have a go. I'm willing to try anything.
(*All sing, except Slap. Pause.*)

Tickle Oh well, that doesn't seem to have done any good. I give up. There's nothing left to do.

Rep (*Off stage.*) Let go of me! I'm going to save the lighthouse!

(*Rep enters and everyone cheers.*)

Tickle Rep! You've come back. The song did work! (*Thumbs up to the children.*) Now we'll be saved from the black hole! ('*Not the . . .!*')

Slap How did you manage to get out? Nobody's ever come back from the black hole! ('*Not the . . .!*')

Rep Well, I told you about the super-duper-dark-shattering light I've got. I just used that. Works wonders! 'Specially when you sing that song.

Albert Er, Rep, I've been thinking about that super-duper-dark-shattering light. I think I'd like to have it here in the lighthouse.

Rep You've changed your mind, have you?

Albert Yes, is it too late?

Rep Never too late to change your mind.

Rep Oh, good. Well, er, could you go and plug it in now, please?

Rep Aren't you forgetting something?

Albert Oh, yes. I suppose you want these.
(*Hands over keys.*)

Rep Thanks. Right, I won't be long!

Tickle Where are you going?

Rep To plug you in.

Tickle Oh, great! It'll be all light again!
(*Exit Rep.*)

Slap Oh, drat! It'll be all light again!

Albert Which reminds me, Slap. What have you got to say for yourself?

Slap Well, Albert, actually I didn't mean all that. I was only joking.

Albert Joking, my eye! You'll get what you deserve now! I'll not have you in my lighthouse a moment longer. Be off with you where you belong – into the black hole! ('*Not the* . . .!')
(*Albert pushes Slap.*)

Slap No, Albert! Don't make me . . . Aagh . . .!

Albert Well, that's got rid of him! And good riddance! Right, Tickle we're just waiting for the super-duper-dark-shattering light and we'll be safe.
(*Rep returns.*)

Rep Well that's just about done it. A few more seconds. Want to count down with me? 5–4–3–2–1–*flash*.
(*Lights flash.*)

Albert Hey, that's great! No more black hole. ('*Not the* . . .!') No more worries!

Tickle Makes me feel like singing!

(*Glad enters.*)

Glad Everyone join in!
(*Sing lighthouse song.*)
(*Exit all.*)

THE END

Family Event

A family service should take place on the Sunday following the holiday club. However, if you believe the family and friends of those children who have attended LIGHT FACTORY would not be tempted to come to 'church', hold it at some other time. A good time would be on the closest weekday evening or Saturday after the end of LIGHT FACTORY. There are some alternative suggestions at the end of this section for those who believe it would be more constructive to have something more informal than a 'service'.

The purpose is to give everyone a taste of the LIGHT FACTORY. This means that there will be an opportunity for the children's family and friends to participate and be part of some of the regular features of LIGHT FACTORY. Therefore, the pattern for the family service event is a shorter version of what the children have been doing throughout the week, with all the major elements included.

All the essential parts of LIGHT FACTORY should be in place. The set, presenters, band, lighting and factory units should be as they have been all week. When family and friends arrive, they should join their children's family unit with their supervisors. A wordsquare (see illustration) should be available for each unit to do in small groups of three or four.

Family Service Programme

Light Factory Song

5 mins The presenters and everyone who knows it sing the song. Repeat so that visitors can join in.

Walk on

1 min The character; the blind man in John 9:1–12; 35–41. He should be dressed in worn, traditional middle-eastern dress and walk across the stage with hands outstretched and eyes closed.

Explain
Get Lit Go

2 mins Tell everyone that during the week when the children have heard a particular signal (demonstrate), each factory unit has done a quick activity. Today's activity is for each unit to quickly stand in a circle and repeat this tongue twister as fast as possible, in turn, and then sit down again. 'Lovely little lights like licking luscious lemon lollies.'

Wordsquare

5 mins Put the answers to the wordsquare on the overhead projector. Mention how each of the words has some relevance to the LIGHT FACTORY. Alternatively, ask the children to put up their hands and explain the relevance of the answers.

Songs

7 mins Sing some of the children's favourite songs from the week.

Walk on

1 min The blind man (as before).

Laser Challenge

10 mins Draw names as usual, but ask for two visitor volunteers. The activity involves working in pairs. One person is blindfolded. The presenters explain that one member of the pair will lead the other through a maze of eggs (which is shown before the blindfolds are put on). The idea is not to break the eggs. While the person is blindfolded, the eggs are replaced with cream crackers, which of course get broken. The sound is almost identical to that of breaking eggs. The audience should be encouraged to give suitable reactions. (The floor should, of course, be covered with newspaper.)

Interview

7 mins One presenter interviews Glad, the cleaner, from the drama serial. The idea is to find out what happened at the Lighthouse. Suitable questions would be, 'Who are you?', 'Where do you work?', 'Has anything interesting happened there recently?'

Get Lit Go

3 mins Sound the signal!

Spotlights

15 mins The blind man walks on, this time shouting, 'I can see'. The presenter should ask him who he is, and what has happened since last time we saw him. This gives him the opportunity to talk about how some people thought that doing wrong had caused his blindness. The blind man can also comment on how surprised everyone was when he could see again. The presenter can now make a comment about the relationship between faith and sight. Just as the blind man needed Jesus to heal him in order to be able to see, so we need Jesus to help us to understand about God. This is a bit like seeing something for the first time. When we begin to know Jesus, we see what God is like. Where Jesus is, there is light. He was light for the blind man and he can be light for us. (John 9:5).

Light Factory Song

4 mins Close the LIGHT FACTORY by singing the song and giving out any appropriate notices.

WORDSEARCH

Find the following words connected with LIGHT FACTORY. You can go up, down, backwards, forwards and diagonally.

JESUS	OVERTIME
LAZARUS	PETER
UNITS	WOMAN
HATS	SPOTLIGHT
LIGHTHOUSE	BLACKHOLE.

A L G T D W O M A N E I K
L Z E L O H K C A L B S B
A U T E F C E Y S R N U Z
Z H B E I M G L P C A S O
A G L I G H T H O U S E P
R P V F A A O A T M P J O
U H B H C T K U L S O A V
S I X W I S A F I R W S E
O P S X R M L V G Z X T R
C M U E O D N J H J O W T
E S T I N U D K T Y U A I
I E O F I O U Y I R J L M
P G E O V H B N E U Z K E

Alternative Event

As an alternative, hold the LIGHT FACTORY at a time other than Sunday and extend it into an 'event'. A good way to do this would be to ask each factory unit to prepare their own game or sport on the final day of LIGHT FACTORY. Simple things, such as guessing how many paper clips there are in a jar, fishing with a magnet, ten pin bowling with empty cans and a sponge ball etc. Family and other visitors could be given thirty minutes to try out these sports before taking part in the 'LIGHT FACTORY' programme. It could also be followed with food and drink prepared by the units, or a 'family' picnic outdoors.

RACE THRO
SKYWALKERS
PLUTO
NEPTUNE
URANUS
SATURN
JUPITER
MARS
EARTH
VENUS
MERCURY
LAUNCH
PAD

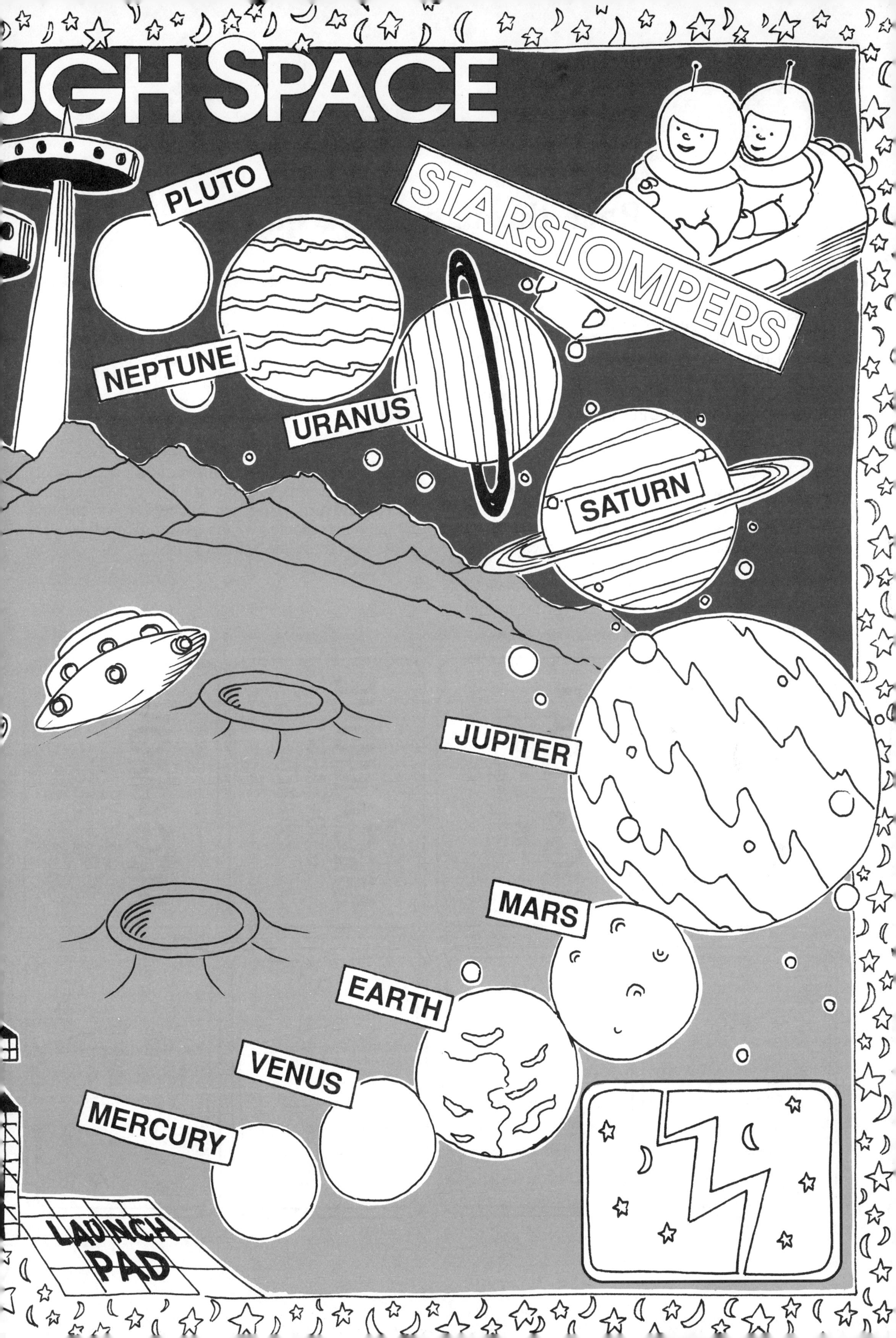
UGH SPACE
PLUTO
STARSTOMPERS
NEPTUNE
URANUS
SATURN
JUPITER
MARS
EARTH
VENUS
MERCURY
LAUNCH PAD

Race through space quiz

The object of the quiz is to get to the lighthouse. Divide the workers into two teams. Questions are asked of the teams alternately. One worker is chosen to give the answer. If the worker answers correctly he/she then picks up a card from the stack of ten. On the reverse side of these cards is:

Two cards – Light leap (move ahead 1 planet)
Four cards – Megamove (move ahead 2 planets)
One card – Hyperspeed (move ahead 3 planets)
Two cards – Captured by Aliens (move back 1 planet)
One card – The black hole – (move back 2 planets)

Spaceships are used for markers.

That team's spaceship should move according to the instructions on the reverse of their card. Play continues until one team gets to the lighthouse. If the worker gets the answer wrong the question goes to the other team.

After being given the opportunity to answer the question, regardless if the answer is correct or incorrect, play remains with this team as it is now technically their turn. After two attempts at any question the presenter should give the answer. The winners are those who get to the lighthouse first.

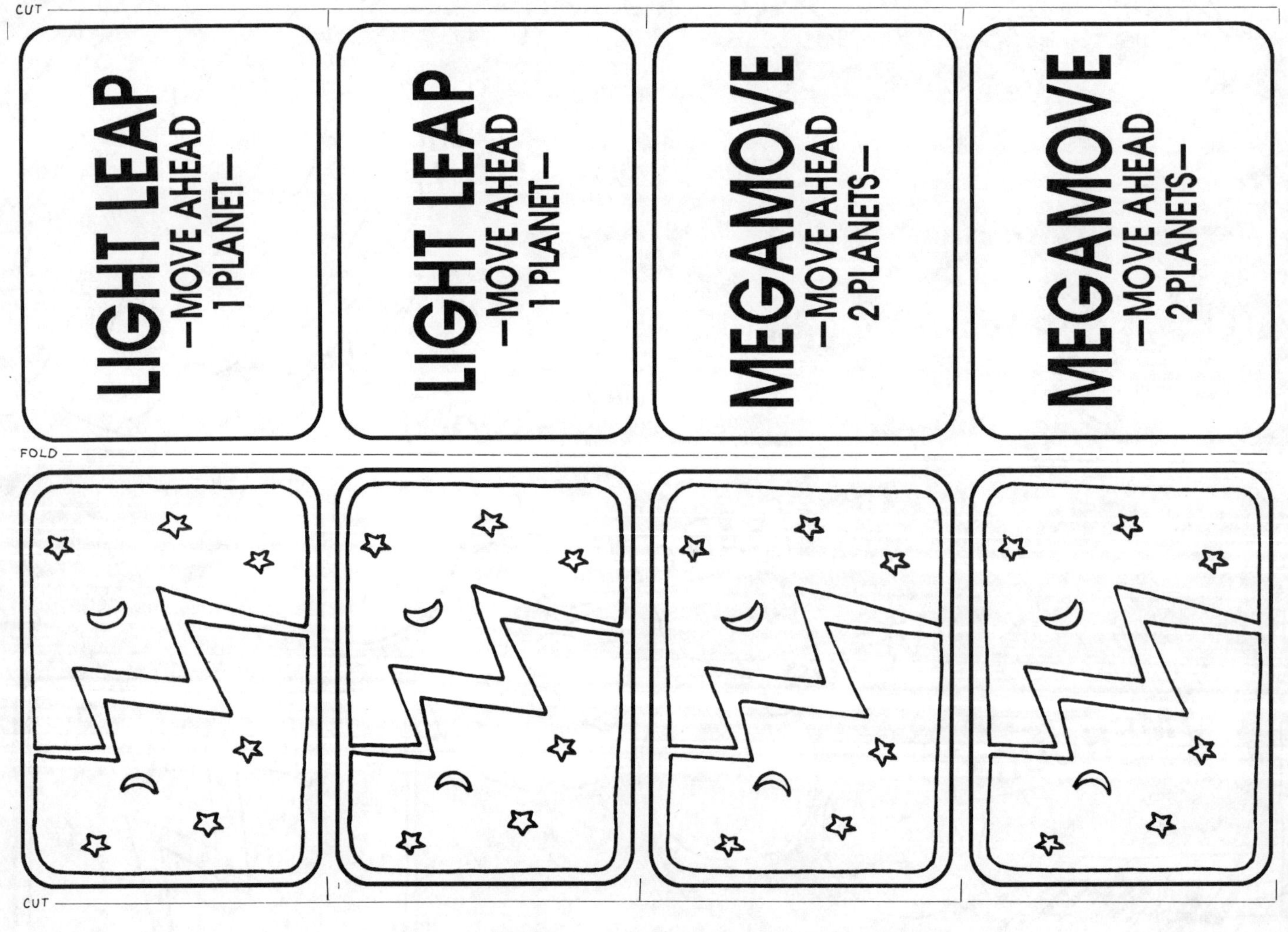

Copy the quiz board on pages 56/57 by photocopying, enlarging, or redrawing larger and colouring.
Photocopy the artwork on these pages and stick the copy onto thin card.
Cut out the cards along the thin black guidelines.
Fold along the dotted foldmarks and stick the two halves together.
Make up the space ship markers as shown below, cutting out the spaceships, mounting onto card and slotting into the stands.
Colour in the cards and markers.

CUT

THE BLACK HOLE
—MOVE BACK
2 PLANETS—

CAPTURED BY ALIENS
—MOVE BACK
1 PLANET—

FOLD

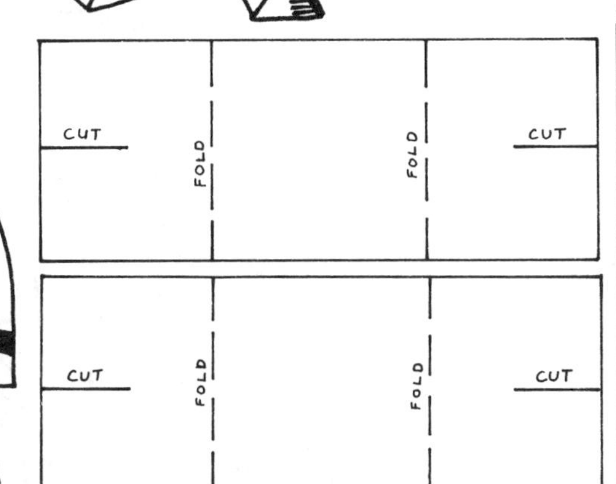

CUT

MEGAMOVE
—MOVE AHEAD
2 PLANETS—

MEGAMOVE
—MOVE AHEAD
2 PLANETS—

HYPERSPEED
—MOVE AHEAD
3 PLANETS—

CAPTURED BY ALIENS
—MOVE BACK
1 PLANET—

FOLD

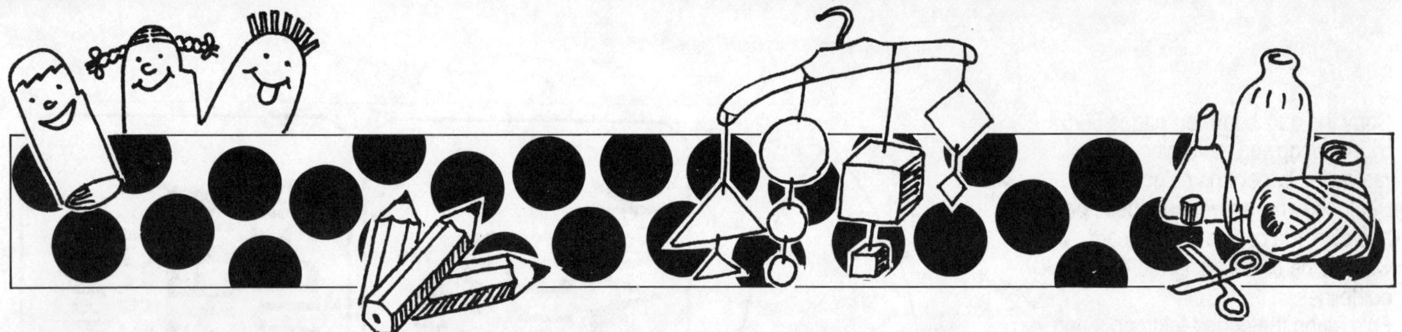

Crafts, Games & Activities

5–7s

Finger puppets
Make these with paper and glue and decorate with felt pens or crayons.

Lollystick puppets
Make these with lollysticks, glue, paper, wool and other materials.

Playdough models
To make your own playdough mix 3 lbs of flour, 1 lb of salt, 1¼ pints of water. Add food colouring, knead well and store. (Lasts about one week.)

Masks
Make these with paper plates and elastic bands, and decorate them with felt pens, crayons, wool and various other materials attached with glue and Sellotape.

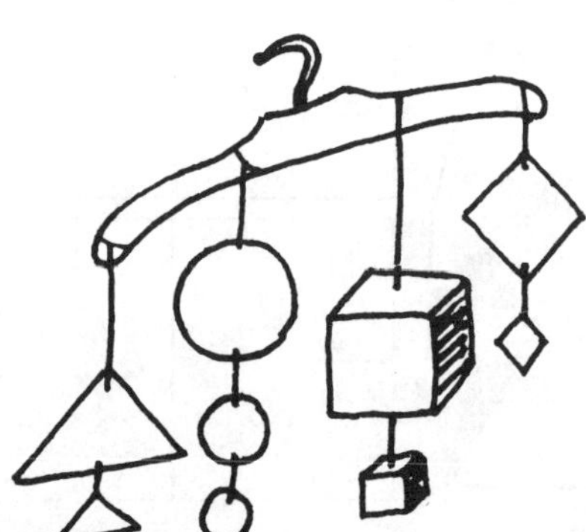

Mobiles
Make these with coat hangers, string and card. Decorate them using felt pens or crayons. (For safety reasons it is best to use plastic coat hangers.)

Wool hunt
Scatter or hide 5″ lengths of wool over a large area and give the children a limited amount of time to find as many of them as possible. When time is up tie the bits together to see how long the wool is all joined together.

Crafts, Games & Activities 7-11s

Mosaic pictures
Make these from paper and various other materials glued onto stiff card.

Junk models
Make these with various containers and materials, put together with glue and Sellotape and painted with poster paints.

Masks
Make these with paper bags. Decorate them with felt pens and various glued-on materials.

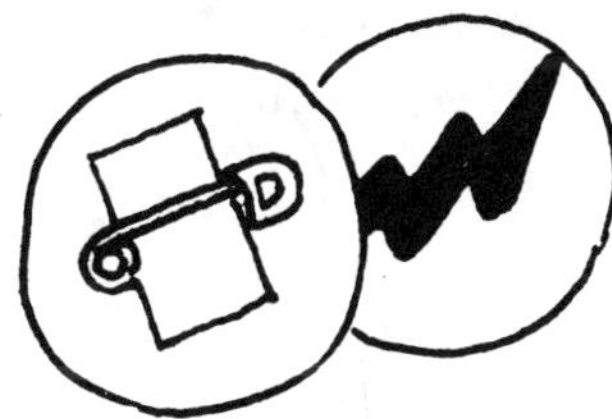

Badges
These can be made from stiff card decorated with felt pens. Stick a safety-pin to the back with Sellotape.

Origami
Books on this, the art of paper-folding, can be found in your local library.

Wordsearch
Using the letters in the words LIGHT FACTORY the children are to find an object beginning with each of those letters and write them on a piece of paper. They should be given a time limit and it is often helpful to them to work in pairs.

Magazine clips
Cut pictures out of magazines and place on the wall only a portion of each picture. The children then have to go around and in a limited amount of time guess what each picture is. When time is up, put the parts up to complete the pictures and let the children see if they got them right.

Crafts, Games & Activities 11-14s

For this age group it is best to offer a variety of activities from which they can choose. Here are some suggestions.

Video corner
Set up a corner where they can go to watch short videos suitable for this age range.

Computer games area
Set up a variety of computer and electronic games to choose from.

Reading area
Have a variety of magazines and books available here.

Drama or art workshop
Could be repeated each day or last the entire week.

Photostory
Suggest that the young people write a story (perhaps dealing with a particular issue or a modern day version of a Bible story). Take photos to illustrate the story and display on stiff card with captions.

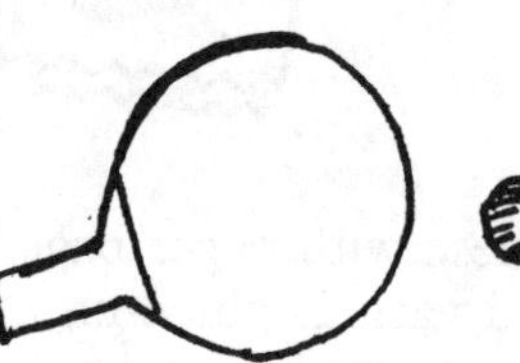

Sports
For those who enjoy sports you could arrange rounders, football, relay games, etc.

Resources

Useful books

Over 300 games for all occasions (Patrick Goodland, SU)
Jesus loves me (SU)
Journey into life (Norman Warren, Falcon)
Find out; A Bible reading aid for 5–7s (SU)
Quest and *Quest Starter*; Bible reading aids for 7–11s (SU)
One to One and *One to One Starter*; Bible reading aid for 10–13s (SU)
Come and Sing (SU)
Junior Praise (Marshall Pickering)
Would you like to know Jesus? A full-colour booklet explaining the basics of Christian belief to under-eights, in words and pictures they can understand (SU).

Light Factory Cassette

A cassette, featuring the Light Factory song and a variety of other songs suitable for this holiday club, is obtainable *only* from the Scripture Union Missions Department. Send your order, with remittance of £5.00 including P&P, to: Missions Department, Scripture Union, 130 City Road, London EC1V 2NJ.

Scripture Union has evangelists all over England and Wales, who work alongside churches, with children and teenagers. They can help you prepare your own holiday club, or come and lead one for you. For further information contact Missions Department, Scripture Union, 130 City Road, London EC1V 2NJ.

Teaching follow-up

You may have had many new children join with your regular group for this holiday club. How are you going to cater for their spiritual needs throughout the rest of the year? You may like to investigate the following teaching materials, which provide an all-year-round programme for the whole church family.

TEACHING MATERIALS FOR CHILDREN UP TO 13+ YEARS

SALT: 3 to 4+ Linked leaflet: *Sparklers.*
SALT: 5 to 7+ Linked leaflet: *All Stars.*
SALT: 8 to 10+ Linked leaflet: *Trailblazers.*
SALT: 11 to 13+ Linked magazine: *Lazer.*
Material for all four age-groups is closely integrated, linked with the church's year and based on a four-year dated syllabus. There is a common theme and aim for each week, with different objectives and programme material for each age-group. Teacher's 'Bible Focus' notes are the same for each age-group. The manuals listed above provide a 30–35 minute 'core' programme for each week, together with additional activities for those with a longer session or for use at other times (an occasional Saturday, a club-night, etc).

SALT: All ages

A quarterly magazine for ministers, co-ordinators and superintendents of children's groups. It includes suggestions for worship for all ages, 'family service' talks, questions for adult groups, sermon outlines, ideas for small groups of 3–13+ – all linked in an integrated syllabus.

RESOURCE MATERIAL

In addition to the SALT material, Scripture Union publish several activity-based resource books. These books are structured around topics and themes, and are ideal for mid-week groups and school clubs.
Splash, by Christine Orme and Christine Wood is for use with under-fives.
Springboard, edited by Sue Clutterham and Denise Trotter, is for use with 7–11s.
Launchpad, edited by Sue Clutterham, is for use with 10–13+.

Bible-reading follow-up

Why not encourage the children to carry on reading the Bible after the holiday club? Scripture Union Bible reading notes (listed above in the 'Resources' section) are carefully geared to meet the needs and capture the interest of children and young people. Help the children in your church to discover what is in them and how to use them. Take a few minutes each week to help them talk with you and with each other about the new things they have been finding out.